James Spencer Northcote

A Visit to the Roman Catacombs

James Spencer Northcote

A Visit to the Roman Catacombs

ISBN/EAN: 9783744675727

Printed in Europe, USA, Canada, Australia, Japan

Cover: Foto ©Andreas Hilbeck / pixelio.de

More available books at **www.hansebooks.com**

A VISIT

TO THE

ROMAN CATACOMBS.

Ballantyne Press
BALLANTYNE, HANSON AND CO.
EDINBURGH AND LONDON

A VISIT

TO THE

ROMAN CATACOMBS.

BY

REV^d J. SPENCER NORTHCOTE, D.D.
CANON OF BIRMINGHAM.

LONDON: BURNS AND OATES.
1877.
[All rights reserved.]

PREFACE.

My study of the Roman Catacombs began in 1846. Two years later I published a series of letters upon the subject in the *Rambler*, and the substance of these, with some additions and corrections, was collected into a small volume in 1856. This was translated both into French and German, and a second English edition was published in 1859.

But in 1864 and 1867 the first two volumes of De Rossi's great work appeared; and these not only added indefinitely to our knowledge of particulars about the Catacombs, but also effected a complete revolution in the view to be taken of their history, and laid a new basis for the future study of them. Formerly, it had been taken for granted that the Christians had had recourse to this mode of burying their dead, only for the sake of the opportunities of secrecy which it afforded, and it was a difficult question for Christian archæologists to solve how it had been possible to carry on a work of such magnitude, under the very eyes (as it were) of the Pagan authorities, without detection. De Rossi set aside these speculations, and proved that there was no necessity for the early Christians to take exceptional precautions with reference to the burial of their dead, since many of the customs of their Pagan neighbours in this matter were such as they might themselves make use of, and, under ordinary circumstances, their cemeteries were adequately protected by the law.

Henceforward, the manual of 1859 was not only incomplete, it had also been demonstrated to be incorrect. In 1869, therefore, a much larger volume was published by Rev. W. R. Brownlow and myself, founded upon the new discoveries. This also was favourably received by the public; the first English edition was soon exhausted, and translations were made both in France and Germany. A second and enlarged edition is now in course of preparation, which will embody the most interesting and important parts of De Rossi's third volume, which has only just appeared. Meanwhile, however, there is need of a short manual, which shall be a safe guide to those who only desire to become acquainted with the leading features of the subject, according to the present condition of our knowledge of it; and with this view I have compiled the following pages, at a time when ill health has necessitated the suspension of more arduous labours. They do not pretend to give a complete account either of the past history or present condition of the Catacombs, but merely a correct outline of the whole, so that those who would pursue the study further shall, at least, have nothing to unlearn.

I have called the volume "A visit to the Roman Catacombs," because it describes the principal objects of interest which are to be seen in the visit now usually paid by educated travellers to the Catacomb of St. Callixtus. To this, however, I have prefixed half a dozen chapters, which make, in fact, three-fourths of the whole work, and in which I have condensed the information which every visitor ought to have before he descends into these subterranean crypts. Unless he has some general idea of what the Catacombs really are, how they came to be made, when and how they were used, and what they contain, he will derive but little pleasure or profit from what he sees in them. I hope, therefore, that this volume will not only be a valuable guide to those who are able to visit the Catacombs, but also a useful introduction to the whole subject for all classes. Those who desire to study it more profoundly must have recourse to De Rossi's learned volumes, or to the English abridgment of them.

ST. DOMINIC'S, STONE, *September* 1877.

P.S.—Any profits derived from the sale of this book will be sent to Commendatore de Rossi to promote the work of excavation, which languishes for want of funds. At more than one spot in the Catacombs, the Commission of Sacred Archæology, of which De Rossi is Secretary, has the strongest reason for believing in the existence of historic monuments of great value, and it is most desirable that these monuments should be recovered, whilst we have amongst us so competent an interpreter of them. But funds are wanting. The late Monsignor de Merode was a most munificent benefactor to this work, and his death has been an irreparable loss. Smaller contributions, however, will be thankfully received; and through the kindness of friends, or by means of my own public lectures, I have been able to send two or three hundred pounds within the last few years. Any further sums that may be intrusted to me for the same purpose will be at once forwarded to Rome.

J. S. N.

TABLE OF CONTENTS.

Part I.

CHAPTER I.

ORIGIN OF THE CATACOMBS.

PAGE

St. Jerome's description of the Catacombs—More detailed description of their galleries, chambers, and tombs; their depth, extent, and number—They were not deserted sand-pits or quarries, but made expressly to be places of burial for Christians—This shown to have been rendered easy by the Roman laws and practice about burial—Pagan burial-clubs in Rome—Perfect freedom and safety of the Christian cemeteries in the beginning 1

CHAPTER II.

THEIR HISTORY DURING THE AGES OF PERSECUTION.

Earliest places of Christian worship in Rome—Their position before the law—Edict of Valerian against assemblies in the Catacombs—Disobedience and consequent martyrdom of St. Sixtus—Extension of the Catacombs—Changes in their architectural forms—The *fossors* and their clerical character—Stories of martyrs belonging to this period—St. Hippolytus and others—SS. Chrysanthus and Daria—St. Tharsicius—St. Agnes and St. Emerentiana 26

CHAPTER III.

THEIR HISTORY FROM A.D. 310 TO A.D. 850.

Gradual disuse of burial in the Catacombs—Other cemeteries not subterranean—Purchase of graves, especially near the tombs of saints—Basilicas built over some of these—Work of Pope Damasus and of Furius Dionysius Filocalus—Burials ceased in the Catacombs in 410—Injuries inflicted by the Goths—Restorations by subsequent Popes—Fresh injuries by the Lombards—Consequent translations of the bodies of the Saints, and gradual neglect of the Catacombs—Those only were visited to which churches or monasteries were attached, especially the cemetery *ad Catacumbas*, which has now given its name to the rest 41

CHAPTER IV.

THEIR LOSS AND RECOVERY.

Catacombs lost sight of for 700 years, accidentally recovered in 1578—Labours and scientific method of Bosio imperfectly followed by his successors—Revival of interest in the subject through Father Marchi, S.J.—Commendatore G. B. de Rossi 51

CHAPTER V.

THEIR PAINTINGS AND SCULPTURE.

Primitive Christian art almost a new subject of Christian archæology—Most of the paintings in the Catacombs, and the best of them, belong to the first four centuries—Resemblance between the most ancient specimens and cotemporary works of Pagan art—Pagan forms of ornamentation freely used, but Christian subjects—The Good Shepherd—Peculiarities in the mode of treatment—Symbolical character of early Christian art; examples, the anchor, lamb, dove, fish—Typical representations of Baptism and the Holy Eucharist, followed by the Resurrection, in the Sacramental chapels of St. Callixtus—Biblical subjects, Noe, Jonas, &c.—Representations of Christ and His Apostles, and of His Holy Mother

—Three successive periods in the development of Christian painting before the age of Constantine—Characteristics of each—Sculpture not so freely used by Christians at first—Subjects carved on sarcophagi 61

CHAPTER VI.

THEIR INSCRIPTIONS.

Number and importance of ancient Christian inscriptions—Destruction of very many of them—Preservation of others by the Popes—Points of resemblance to Pagan epitaphs—Points of difference—Absence of any token of social distinctions—Birth of Christian epigraphy—Active love its chief characteristic—Prayer for the dead—Prayer to the Saints—Examples—Other characteristics of later epitaphs—Age—Date of death—Unmeaning titles of praise—Words used to denote death, *in pace, contra votum,* &c. 108

Part II.

CHAPTER I.

THE PAPAL CRYPT.

Entrance to the Cemetery of St. Callixtus—Cemetery above ground—*Graffiti* at entrance of the Papal Crypt—Original epitaphs of several of the Popes of the third century—Inscription by Pope Damasus explained . . . 125

CHAPTER II.

THE CRYPT OF ST. CECILIA.

Ancient notices of burial of St. Cecilia near the Popes—Discovery of the crypt—Description of its ornamentation—Refutation of the claim of the Catacomb at St. Sebastian's to be considered the burial-place of St. Cecilia . . . 139

CHAPTER III.

THE CRYPT OF ST. EUSEBIUS.

Precautions taken by Pope Damasus and others to guide pilgrims to the particular tomb they wished to visit—Copy of the epitaph in honour of St. Eusebius—Fragments of the original set up by Damasus—Important historical revelation to be gathered from it—Discipline of the Church in regard to the *lapsi*—Title of martyr given to Eusebius—Translation of his body 150

CHAPTER IV.

THE TOMB OF ST. CORNELIUS.

St. Cornelius buried in another Catacomb—Objects of interest to be seen *en route*—The family vault of the Deacon Severus at end of third century—Paintings of the Good Shepherd, accompanied by two of His Apostles and several sheep—Of Moses taking off his shoe, striking the rock, &c.—Tomb of St. Cornelius, and its epitaph—Inscriptions above and below it of Popes Damasus and Siricius—Figures of SS. Cornelius and Cyprian; of SS. Sixtus II. and Optatus—Very ancient paintings in two adjacent chambers—Conclusion . . 157

ROMA SOTTERRANEA.

ROMA SOTTERRANEA.

Part First.

CHAPTER I.

THE ORIGIN OF THE CATACOMBS.

THE great St. Jerome, writing about 1500 years ago, tells us that when he was a schoolboy in Rome, he used to go every Sunday, in company with other boys of his own age and tastes, to visit the tombs of the apostles and martyrs, and to go down into the crypts excavated there in the bowels of the earth. "As you enter," he says, "you find the walls on either side full of the bodies of the dead, and the whole place is so dark, that one seems almost to realise the fulfilment of those words of the prophet, 'Let them go down alive into Hades.' Here and there a little light admitted from above suffices to give a momentary relief to the horror of the darkness; but, as you go forward, you find yourself again plunged into the utter blackness of night, and the words of the poet come unbidden to your mind, 'The very silence fills the soul with dread.'" Anybody who has frequented the Roman Catacombs will recognise the justice of this description; and if he is as familiar with Virgil and with the Psalms of David as St. Jerome was, he may have used something like the same language to describe his own impressions. But we are writing for those who have never seen the Catacombs at all, and we must therefore enter into more minute particulars.

Let us first try to get a general idea of what the Catacombs are. And for this purpose let us transport ourselves in imagination to the city of Rome, and having been led out some two or three miles (more or less) almost on any of the fourteen great consular roads which went forth from the old centre of the world to its most distant provinces, let us go down, either by some modern staircase or through some accidental fissure in the soil, into the bowels of the earth. At the depth of fifteen or twenty feet we shall probably find ourselves landed in a dark narrow gallery, something like what is here represented—a gallery about three feet wide, and perhaps seven or eight feet high, cut out of the living rock, and its walls on either side pierced with a number of horizontal shelves, one above the other, like the shelves of a bookcase. We need hardly be told that each of these shelves once contained a dead body, and had then been shut up by long tiles or slabs of marble, securely fastened by cement, and inscribed perhaps with the name of the deceased or with some Christian emblem. Probably some grave still uninjured may

Gallery with Tombs.

lie within our sight, or we may see bones and ashes in some of the graves that are open.

If we step forward and enter one of the doorways to be found on either side, it will introduce us to a small chamber, twelve or fourteen feet square perhaps. If there is nothing but graves cut in the walls of this chamber, just as in the galleries, we may safely conjecture that it was only a family vault. But if we find a bench hewn out of the rock all round the room, together with a chair (or perhaps two) similarly excavated, we can hardly be wrong in supposing that the room was once used as a place of assembly, whether for purposes of public psalmody or of religious instruction. Or, if the principal tomb in the chamber be shaped like an altar, if two or three

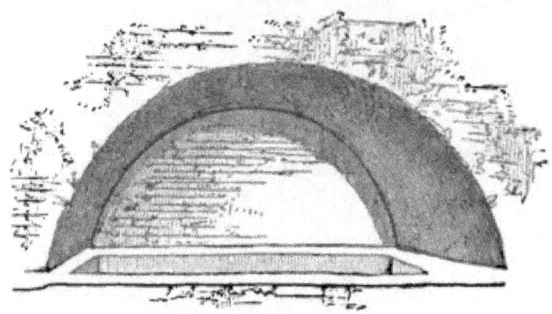

Arcosolium, or altar-shaped tomb.

chambers open out of one another, and if one of these have an absidal termination, with a chair at the end and a low seat running round the sides, such as may still be seen in some of the old basilicas above ground for the accommodation of the bishop and clergy, no one can justly accuse us of rashness if we suspect that we stand in a place that was provided for the celebration of the Christian mysteries in days of persecution.

If we were sufficiently bold to leave the gallery which we first entered, and to pursue our way further into the interior, we should soon lose ourselves in some such labyrinth as is here represented. This diagram is a true map of a small portion (perhaps not more than an eighth) of a catacomb on the Via Nomentana, commonly known by the name of St.

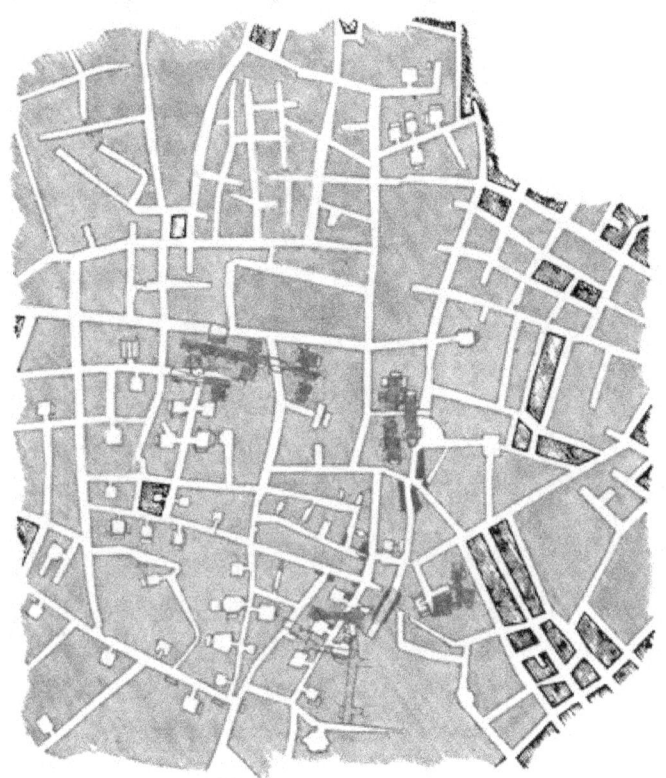

Part of Catacomb of St. Agnes.

Agnes. It is about 230 yards long by 180 in width; yet if all the galleries in this small section of a catacomb were stretched out in one continuous line, they would make very nearly two English miles in length. And then we must remember that in almost all these subterranean cemeteries the same thing is repeated on two or three different levels—in some of them even on five levels. In the Catacomb of St. Callixtus, on the

Via Appia, we can descend by a succession of staircases to five different *stories*, so to speak; and perhaps

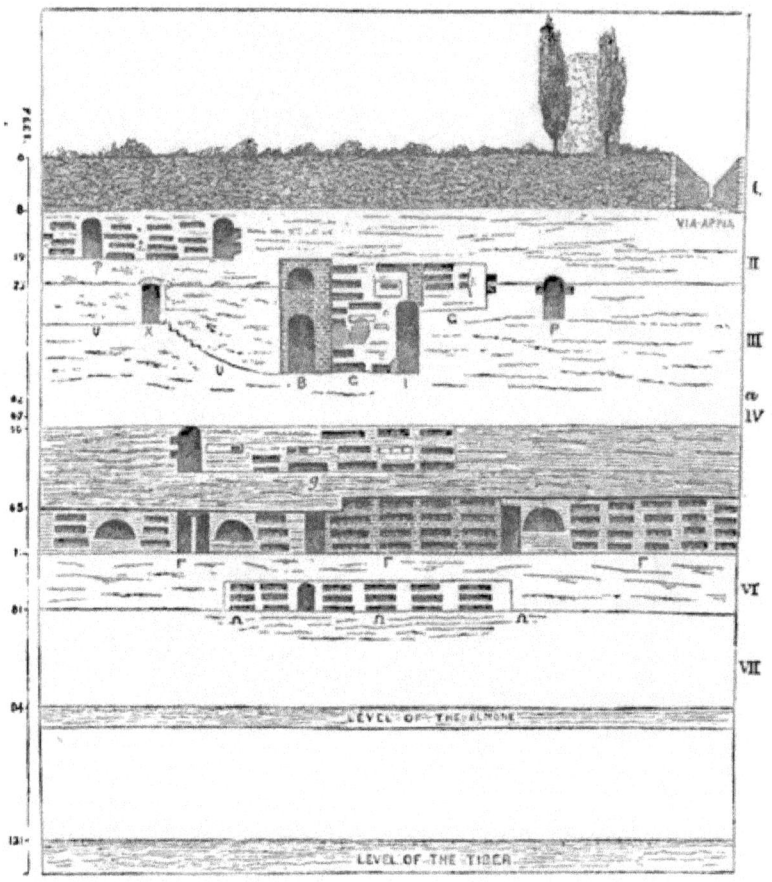

Section of the Cemetery of St. Callixtus.

the excavators might have made even a sixth and a seventh had they not by this time come to the level of water, where any galleries they might dig would soon have become mere subterranean canals.

But we have not even yet finished our tale of

wonder. One such excavation as this would have been a remarkable work, and its history would have deserved examination. But in the hills round Rome there are forty or fifty such, of various sizes indeed, and each having its own name and history, but all evidently inspired by the same idea and forming part of the same general plan. What was this plan? For what purpose were these labyrinths of long narrow galleries and small chambers so laboriously excavated?

To this question their very form seems to supply the only possible answer. They were made to bury the dead. This is undeniably the first and principal use to which they were put. It is no less certain that this was also the object for which they were designed. Time was, indeed, when learned men shrank from this conclusion, and suggested, that though unquestionably they were used as burial-places, yet perhaps this was only an afterthought, and that they may have been originally designed for something else. The building of Rome, it was said, must have required vast quantities of stone and of sand to make cement; perhaps, therefore, in the Roman Catacombs we have only lit upon a certain number of exhausted, or rather deserted, sandpits and quarries, which later generations availed themselves of, for economy's sake, as places of burial.

This theory sounds very plausible at a distance from the places themselves; but on closer examination on the spot there are found fatal objections to it. One is, that they happen not to be excavated either in sand or in stone, but precisely in a rock of intermediate consistency, too solid to be used as sand, too soft and friable to be used as building-stone; and perhaps this might be allowed to stand as a peremptory refutation of the theory in question. But we will add another argument, not less simple or less conclusive, drawn from the different forms of the two kinds of excavation. Compare the subjoined plan with that which has been give before on page 5. These two excavations occur in the same place. They overlie one another on the Via Nomentana, and they are here drawn on precisely the same scale. Could they be mistaken one for the other? Do they look like parts of the same plan? One represents the long, narrow, straight streets or galleries and occasional chambers of a catacomb; the other, the broad, tortuous, and irregular excavations of a sandpit. The makers of both had each a definite object in their work, but these objects were distinct from, and even opposed to, one another; and hence the two systems have distinct, and even contrary, characteristics. The only point in common between them is, that both were carried on underground, and both wished to disturb as little as possible

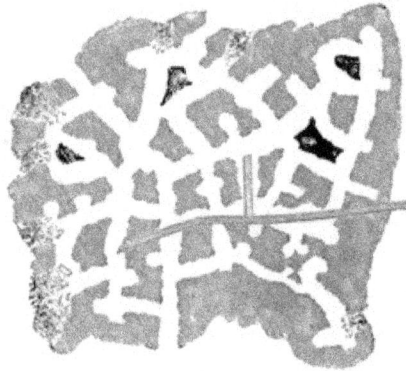

Plan of Arenaria at St. Agnes'.

the superficial soil. But the quarryman aimed at taking out as much of the material as he could, and with the least trouble; whilst the Christian *fossor* desired to extract as little of the material as was consistent with his object of providing hundreds or thousands of graves. Hence we find in the sand-pit broad roads, admitting the use of horses or carts, and these roads well rounded off at the corners for the facility of passing to and fro; whereas the paths of the cemetery cross one another at right angles, that so every part of their walls may be available for purposes of sepulture, whilst they are so narrow that two men can scarcely walk abreast in them. Moreover, in the sandpits the roof is arched, and the vault of the arch springs from the very ground; whereas in the catacombs the walls of the galleries are made strictly perpendicular, in order that horizontal shelves, capable of supporting the bodies of the dead, might be safely cut in them, and the tiles that shut them in might have adequate support. In a word, the two kinds of excavation could hardly be mistaken for one another. A catacomb could only be made to look like a sandpit or quarry by first destroying all the graves, widening the paths, and rounding their angles; in a word, by destroying every characteristic of a catacomb; and a sandpit could be turned into a cemetery resembling the Catacombs, only by setting up such a quantity of masonry as must needs remain to tell its own tale. There are actual examples of this metamorphose to be found in three or four places of the Catacombs; and here is the representation of one of them, from the Catacomb of St. Hermes,

Sections of Gallery in St. Hermes.

on the Via Salara. What an amount of labour and expense was necessary to effect the change, and, after all, with a result how clumsy and unsatisfactory as compared with those places which were excavated directly and primarily for the purpose of burial!—*so* unsatisfactory, indeed, that presently the Christians left off prosecuting the work even here where they had begun it. Though immense spaces of the sand-pit still remained unoccupied, they chose rather to excavate after their own fashion in the virgin rock below. We may conclude, then, without a shadow of doubt, that those excavations which we call the Roman Catacombs were made solely for the sake of burying the dead.

But by whom? and to bury what dead? We answer, and again without hesitation—By Christians, and only to bury Christians. And if it is asked on what authority this statement is made, we might point to the thousands of Christian inscriptions that have been found in them, and to the utter absence of evidence in favour of any other account of them. Our readers, however, would probably insist that it was impossible for the early Christians, a small and persecuted body, going about stealthily and in disguise, as it were, among the Pagan multitude, to have executed so vast a work.

First, let me say—though the remark hardly comes here in its proper place, yet, as it may help to dissipate a prejudice, let me anticipate a little and say—that the work in its full magnitude, such as we have been describing it, was the work (to speak roughly) of three centuries of labour. There is evidence that the Catacombs were used as Christian cemeteries even before the end of the first century, and they certainly continued to be so used, more or less, up to the first decade of the fifth. Among the inscriptions found in them is one of the year of our Lord 72; there are others of 107, 110, and so on, down to 410; so that the whole period of their use includes almost a century of the Church's peace, as well as all the time of her persecution.

However, here as elsewhere the difficulty is not about the end of the work, but about its beginning. How was it possible that the Christians in the first and second centuries could have executed any part of the great work we have described? How could they have made a beginning? how carried it on?

Was it a work done in violation of the law, and therefore in secret? or was it public and notorious, and such as their Pagan neighbours, enemies though they were, could not legitimately interfere with? The answers to these questions are to be sought in learned volumes of old Roman law, and in hundreds of Latin Pagan inscriptions, which, however, cannot be transferred to these pages. For our present purpose their contents may be thus briefly summarised.

It was the common practice of Roman gentlemen and ladies of wealth to make in their wills very minute provisions for their tombs, and for certain rites and ceremonies to be performed at their tombs after death. They ordinarily set apart some portion of a field or garden near the high road, accurately measured off with so many feet of frontage and so many feet into the field behind; and in the middle of this plot they ordered a monument to be erected—often a chamber of considerable dimensions, with an altar of stone or of fine marble in which their bones or ashes should be laid, and benches of the same material, with cushions and all else that was necessary for the convenience of guests, whom they invited to come and partake here of a feast in their memory, both on the anniversary of their death and on several other occasions. The cost of the tomb was often specified in the will, and recorded on the epitaph; and the expenses of the feasts were met partly by contributions from dependants of the deceased who were intended to partake of it, partly by the rent of certain houses or gardens, or by the interest of moneys bequeathed by the deceased himself or by others for this purpose. The execution of this part of the will was commonly intrusted to some one or more faithful freedmen, who had a direct interest in its fulfilment; and heavy fines were inflicted on the heirs in case of neglect.

The motive of these testamentary dispositions is obvious; they were made in the vain hope that by these means the name and memory of the deceased might not utterly perish. And the Roman law did all that it could to secure the realisation of so natural a wish; it fenced every place of burial round about with divers safeguards, and punished its violation with the severest penalties. First of all, the burial of a single corpse (or the deposit of the little urn of ashes if the body had been burnt) sufficed to impart a sort of religious character to the spot where these remains had been laid for their last resting-place, provided the burial had been made with the consent of the owner of the soil. Henceforth that place no longer belonged to the category of ordinary landed property, but became subject to new and peculiar laws of its own. It did not pass by will as part of the inheritance; no prescriptive right had any power to alienate it; if at any time some undutiful descendant should secretly obliterate all visible tokens of its use as a place of burial, and fraudulently effect a sale of the property as though it were common land, the law would interfere to annul the contract as soon as it was discovered, no matter after what lapse of time; it would oblige the purchaser to surrender his purchase, and the vendor or his heirs to make restitution of the purchase-money, together with interest at a very high rate; and the money thus forfeited was devoted to some public use of beneficence. Even this penalty, severe as it is, fell short of what the law prescribed in the case of those who had themselves violated a sepulchre. This was accounted so heinous a crime, that it was punished by banishment or perpetual labour in the mines, according to the condition in life of the offender; and the acts of violation subject to this penalty were such as these:—the breaking open of a sepulchre, the intrusion into it of a stranger's corpse, *i.e.*, of one not belonging to the family, or not included in the list of those to whom the concession was made by the original testator, the carrying away of any stone, pillar, or statue, or even the erasure of an epitaph.

This was the common law of the land in Imperial Rome; and the most remarkable thing about it is this, that, except in times of civil war and great public commotion, it protected the tombs, not only of the rich and noble, but of those whom the law despised or even execrated, such as slaves and criminals. It was specially enacted that the bodies of public malefactors, who had suffered death at the hands of the executioner, were to be given up on the petition of their friends, to be buried where they pleased ; and when once this had been done, the tomb fell under the guardianship of the Pontifices as effectually as any other tomb. Of course, there was occasionally exceptional legislation on this subject, as, for instance, with reference to some of the Christian martyrs ; but these exceptions were rare, and prompted by special reasons; they do not invalidate the general truth of the statements which have been made, nor of the conclusion which may legitimately be drawn from them ; viz., that at the very time when the Roman law was most severe against Christianity as a religion, aiming at nothing short of its extinction, this same law would, nevertheless, have extended its protection to Christian cemeteries, if there were any.

And how should there not have been ? For Christians died like other folk, and had need to be buried ; and what was to hinder some wealthy "brother" from giving up some portion of a field of his, in as public a situation as he pleased—indeed, the nearer to the high road, the more closely would it be in accordance with the practice of his Pagan neighbours —and allowing his Christian brethren to be buried there ? He might confine the use of it, if he would, to members of his own family, or he might make it common to all the faithful, or he might fix whatever other limits he pleased to its use. He might also build on the ground some house or chamber, or conspicuous monument; he might assign as much land as he chose all round it for its support; and underneath this house and land the work of excavation might proceed without let or hindrance; there was no need of concealment, and there is no proof that at the first commencement of the Church any concealment was attempted.

On the contrary, the tendency of all modern discoveries has been in the opposite direction. Now that we have learnt to distinguish one part of a cemetery from another, and to trace the several periods of their excavation in chronological order, it has been made clear that each several part was originally a separate *area* as well defined as that of any Pagan monument, and its limits, like theirs, were determined by the course of the adjacent road, and walls of enclosure built for the purpose. We find, for example, that what is now called the Catacomb of St. Callixtus, is made up of eight or ten such *areæ*, each with its own staircase, and its own system of excavation, conducted with order and economy. The *area* that was first used here for purposes of Christian burial measured 250 Roman feet by 100, and its galleries were reached by two staircases, entering boldly from the surface, within sight of all passers-by along the Appian Way, and going straight to their point. By and by, a second *area* was added of the same dimensions; and in process of time, a third, 150 feet by 125; a fourth, of the same dimensions, and so on.

The internal arrangements of some of these *areæ* have undergone so much change in the course of centuries, that it is no longer possible to recover the precise form of their original entrances. But what is not found in one place is found in another; and one of the recent discoveries has been the entrance to a famous catacomb on the Via Ardeatina, not far from the cemetery of which we have just been speaking

Entrance to a most Ancient Christian Sepulchre at Tor Marancia.

It is cut in the side of a hill close to the highway and has a front of very fine brickwork, with a cornice of terra-cotta, and the usual space for an inscription, which has now unfortunately perished. The sepulchre to which it introduces us is ornamented with Christian paintings of a very classical character; and it may be considered as proved that it once belonged to the Flavian family,—that imperial family which gave Vespasian to the throne, and (as we learn even from Pagan authors) gave a martyr and several confessors to the Christian Church. The cemetery was begun in the days of Domitian, *i.e.*, towards the end of the first century, and it is known by the name of his relative, St. Domitilla, on whose property (there is good reason to believe) it was excavated. The entrance is flanked on either side by a chamber, built of brick subsequently to the excavation of the subterranean sepulchre. The larger of these chambers, with the bench running all the way round it, was evidently the place of meeting for those whose duty or privilege it was to assemble here on the appointed anniversaries to do honour to the deceased; the smaller space, on the left, with its well and cistern, and fragments of a staircase, was no less obviously occupied by the dwelling-house of the *custode*, or guardian of the monument.

We have said that the inscription has perished, but we can see where it once was, and we can supply a specimen of such an inscription from other catacombs; *e.g.*, it might have been simply SEPULCRUM FLAVIORUM, like the EUTYCHIORUM lately discovered in the Catacomb of St. Callixtus, or it might have been longer and more explicit, like the inscription found in the cemetery of St. Nicomedes, found a few years ago on the other side of Rome. Not far from the entrance of this cemetery there lay a stone which declared to whom the monument belonged, viz., to one Valerius Mercurius and Julitta (who was

probably his wife); then another gentleman is named, and one or two ladies, and finally their freedmen and freedwomen; but this important condition is added, AD RELIGIONEM PERTINENTES MEAM,—"if they belong to my religion." It is true there is no Christian emblem on this stone to declare the faith of the writer, but the cemetery in which it is found is undeniably Christian; and among the thousands or tens of thousands of Pagan inscriptions that have come down to us, we do not find one that contains the remarkable expression I have quoted. Indeed, it is doubtful whether it would have had any meaning to Pagan ears; but a Christian or a Jew would have understood it well. And it reminds us of another very ancient inscription which may yet be seen in the Catacomb of St. Domitilla, where it served to appropriate a particular chamber as the family vault of its owner. The inscription runs in this wise:—
"M. Aurelius Restutus made this subterranean chamber for himself and those of his family who believe in the Lord."

Our limited space will not allow us to produce further evidence of the liberty and publicity of the Christian cemeteries in their beginning; but further evidence ought not to be required, since there is really none whatever on the other side. It cannot be shown that the Roman Government ever interfered with the Catacombs before the middle of the third century, and not even then with reference to their original and more ordinary use as places of burial, but rather to a later but very important use to which they were then being put—as places of assembly and religious worship.

There is one objection, however, to our argument which cannot be passed over in silence—it will doubtless have already suggested itself to some of our readers. They will have called to mind the testimony of St. Paul, that not many mighty, not many noble, were among the first disciples of the faith, and therefore that what was possible for a Flavius Clemens, a Domitilla, or a Cecilia, was nevertheless quite beyond the reach of the humbler and more numerous part of the Christian community. Most true; but there is abundant evidence to show that burial of the dead was considered one of the highest works of Christian charity, in which the rich accounted it a duty and a pleasure to aid the poor. Moreover, where the work was not done by wealthy individuals, it might easily have been done by means of an association of numbers, and this too would have been protected by the law.

Under the laws of the old Roman Republic, there was scarcely any limit to the exercise of the right of association among its citizens; but from the days of Julius Cæsar private clubs or corporations (*collegia*) were looked upon with grave suspicion, and the right of meeting was but sparingly granted by the Senate or the Emperor. We have a notable example of this suspicion in the refusal by the Emperor Trajan of a petition from his friend and trusted official, Pliny. Pliny had asked for leave to form in one of the towns of his province a body of firemen, 150 in number, and assured his imperial master that he would be careful in his selection of men, and vigilant over their conduct. But Trajan peremptorily refused, on the plea of political mischief, which (he said) experience showed to be the ordinary fruit even of associations apparently most harmless. One important exception, however, was made to this policy of stern repression. It was permitted to the poorer classes to form clubs for the purpose of providing for the expenses of their burial, and they were allowed to meet once a month to pay their contributions, and to make the necessary regulations for the management of their affairs with a view to the attainment of this object. An immense number of most curious and interesting monuments still survive, showing how largely the Roman poor availed themselves of this privilege in the second and third centuries of our era, and what sound practical sense they exhibited in establishing the laws and conditions of membership in these burial-clubs. It is a most tempting field, upon which, however, we must not dwell at any length. We can only call attention to the language of Tertullian in a work especially addressed to the Roman Government, and in which, using almost the very words of the law on the subject of these clubs, he explains how Christians on a certain day of the month make voluntary contributions for certain benevolent purposes, of which he specifies the burial of the dead as one.

We cannot doubt, therefore, that as some of the Roman Catacombs may have been the private work, and even remained the private property, of individuals or families, so others, possibly from the first, certainly as early as the end of the second century, belonged to the Christian community collectively, and were administered for the general good by dulyappointed officers. The earliest instance of this, of which any written evidence has come down to us, is the cemetery of which we have already spoken on the Via Appia, and which was intrusted by Pope Zephyrinus to the care of his archdeacon, Callixtus, whose name it has ever since retained. A monument may yet be seen in it showing how, a century later, this same cemetery still remained under the immediate jurisdiction of the Pope, and was administered by his deacon; for this was the arrangement made. The bishops were the legal possessors of the cemeteries, churches, and other religious places; but it was well understood, and the very language of the imperial decrees often acknowledges, that they really belonged to the whole body of the Christians, and not to any private individual; and the deacons acted as the *quæstores*, or representatives and agents of the body.

It was not necessary that the Christians should obtain any special leave to form a *collegium*, nor seek for any special privileges. The ordinary liberties of every Roman citizen were sufficient for their purpose. Most of the Pagan burial-clubs indeed had, or pretended to have, a certain religious character, being usually placed under the invocation of some one or other of the gods. But this was not an essential condition of their existence. It was not necessary, therefore, that the Christians should put forward any religious profession at all, nor even take the name of a *collegium*. They might have retained, and probably did retain, their own favourite and characteristic name of *Fratres*; and, provided the ostensible motive of their association was to provide the means of burial for their members, they might have held meetings and possessed property with impunity. In this way a sort of practical *modus vivendi* was established for them under the reign of the more just and merciful Emperors. The religious character of their meetings, though well known, might yet be winked at, so that they were tolerated, just as many Egyptian, Greek, and Asiatic religious confraternities (*erani*, or *thiasi*), were not interfered with so long as they gave no umbrage to the Government; and the laws which forbade the profession of the Christian religion were at those times restricted in their application to individual cases of accusation as they arose, just as we know that Trajan at least had enjoined. Nevertheless, those laws still remained; and when the hour of persecution came, the charge of practising a *religio illicita* could be insisted upon, and all Christian meetings forbidden.

Let us now briefly sum up what has been said, and see what light it throws on the origin of the Roman Catacombs. It has been shown that the habits of Pagan Rome about burials and burial-grounds, during the first centuries of the Christian era, unconsciously, yet most effectively, shielded the work of the infant Church. The extensive *area* so frequently attached to the monuments of the wealthy; the house or chamber built upon it; the assignment of property for its support to chosen friends, with the infliction of fines in case of neglect; the inalienability of any land which had once been used for purposes of burial; the power of admitting friends and excluding strangers by the mere will of the testator; the right of combination, or making clubs, to secure and maintain such burial-places by means of monthly contributions; the habit of visiting the monument, and of eating and drinking there in solemn memory of the departed;—all these facts or principles, guaranteed by Roman law and practice as the privilege of every citizen, were of admirable convenience to the makers and frequenters of the Christian Catacombs. They furnished a real legal screen for the protection of the Christian Society in a matter that was very near their hearts. If a number of Christians were seen wending their way to this or that cemetery, and entering its adjacent *cella*, they would be to Pagan eyes only the members of a burial-club, or the relations, friends, and dependants of some great family going out to the appointed place to celebrate the birthday or some other anniversary of a deceased benefactor ; and if disposed to give evasive answers to inconvenient questions, some perhaps might have even dared to say that such was indeed their errand. It would be noticed, of course, that they did not use the funeral pile; but they could not be molested on this account, since custom only, and not law, prescribed its use. To these objectors they might answer boldly with Minucius Felix, "We follow the better and more ancient custom of burial!" Again, the Pagans might grumble, but they could hardly punish, for neglecting to sprinkle roses or violets on the sepulchres of the dead. But as to the main external features of the case, we repeat that what the Pagans ordinarily did in the way of providing burial-places for their dead was very much the same as what the Christians desired to do; and under the screen of this resemblance the Roman Catacombs began.

CHAPTER II.

THEIR HISTORY DURING THE AGES OF PERSECUTION.

How long the Roman Christians were allowed to bury their dead where they pleased, and to visit their tombs in peace, we can hardly say. In Africa there had been a popular outcry against the Christian cemeteries, and a demand for their destruction, in the beginning of the third century; and the same thing may have happened in Rome also at the same or even at an earlier date. The first certain record, however, of any legal interference with the Roman Catacombs belongs to a period fifty years later, by which time they must have been both numerous and extensive; it must also have been very notorious where they were situated. We have seen how public the entrance was to the Catacomb of St. Domitilla in the first century, and there is no reason to suppose that this was an exception to the general rule. The Cœmeterium Ostrianum, on the Via Nomentana, was as old, and probably as well known, for it was the place where St. Peter had baptized; the Catacomb of St. Priscilla, too, of the noble family of Pudens, on the Via Salara, and several others.

We read of St. Anacletus, who was Bishop of

Rome about A.D. 160, that he built some sort of monument over the tomb of St. Peter on the Vatican, and his predecessors and some few of his successors till the end of the century were buried in this same place, *juxta corpus Beati Petri*, as the old records have it. Around the tomb of St. Paul, also, on the Via Ostiensis, a cemetery was formed, of which a few monuments still remain, bearing dates of the first decade of the second century. Hence a priest, writing in that same century, calls these tombs of the Apostles "the trophies," or triumphal monuments, "of those who had laid the foundation of the Church in Rome." About a hundred years later we read of St. Fabian—Pope A.D. 236-250—that "he caused numerous buildings to be constructed throughout the cemeteries." And this expression seems to imply that the cemeteries were no longer private property (as several of them undoubtedly were at the first), but belonged to the Church in her corporate capacity, and were administered, therefore, under the superintendence of her rulers. We have contemporary evidence that this was the condition of a cemetery on the Via Appia from the beginning of the third century, Pope Zephyrinus having set over it his chief deacon, Callixtus; and the obvious advantages of such an arrangement may have led to its general, if not universal, adoption. At any rate, we cannot doubt that "the numerous buildings he caused to be constructed throughout the cemeteries" were either oratories for public worship, or chambers for the celebration of the *agapæ*, which he caused to be built after the fashion of the *scholæ* of the Pagan burial-clubs, in the *areæ* of cemeteries which had not had them before; and we can easily understand how this increased provision of places for assembly had been rendered necessary by the rapid multiplication of the faithful during the long peace which the Church had enjoyed since the reign of Caracalla.

At the first beginning of the Church in Rome, the Christians had, of course, met together only in private houses, "under cover of that great liberty which invested with a sort of sacred independence the Roman household;" but as their numbers increased, this could not have sufficed. Very early in the third century, therefore, and probably even much earlier, there were places of public Christian worship within the city; and it seems certain that the faithful were allowed also to assemble (at least under ordinary circumstances) in the public *areæ* of their cemeteries up to the middle of the same century. The language of Tertullian, complaining that the heathen "had become acquainted with their days of meeting, and that hence they were continually besieged, betrayed, and caught unawares in their most secret congregations," suggests rather the idea of meetings in subterranean hiding-places than of public assemblies. But he also tells us that some congregations used to purchase immunity to themselves by payment of tribute to the Government, and that for this purpose they were enrolled on the police registers, where, as he takes care to remind them, they found themselves in anything but respectable company. These, of course, must have had public places of meeting; but under what title they can have met, unless it was that of burial-clubs, such as were described in our last chapter, it is not easy to conjecture. They could not be enrolled merely as professors of the Christian faith; for ever since the first persecution by Nero, the Roman Government had persistently refused to give any legal recognition to "the new superstition." For a while, indeed, the Jews and Christians had been regarded as professing the same religion, and this was a great gain to the Christians, for there had been a decree of Cæsar that the Jews throughout the whole Roman Empire should be allowed to keep their ancient customs without let or hindrance. The Jews themselves soon vigorously denounced their supposed co-religionists, and when Christianity had once established its independence of Judaism, it fell under the ban of an illicit religion. Thenceforward, though the Christians were not always being persecuted, they were always liable to persecution, so that even when it was forbidden to accuse them, yet, if they were brought before justice and acknowledged themselves Christians, it was forbidden to absolve them. This was the state of things under the reign of Aurelian and Commodus, in the latter half of the second century, when we read of a certain senator, named Apollonius, that he was accused of Christianity, and pleading guilty to the charge, was beheaded, while yet the man who had informed against him was condemned to death also, but by the more cruel and ignominious method of breaking on the wheel. The beautiful story of St. Cecilia, too, belongs (it is now ascertained) to some more active period of persecution about this same time. The story need not be repeated here, but one of its details is worth referring to, as it probably gives a true picture of what was happening not unfrequently in those days, viz., that some of the clergy lay hid in the Catacombs, and inquirers after the truth were conducted by trusty guides to their retreat. We must not suppose, however, that any large number of the faithful ever took refuge there for any length of time; indeed, such a thing would have been physically impossible. The Christians assembled there for purposes of worship when the public exercise of their religion was interfered with; and then this secrecy, thus cruelly forced upon them, was cast in their teeth, and they were called "a skulking, darkness-loving people."

At length, in the year 253, Valerian published a decree whereby he sought to close against them even this subterranean retreat; he forbade them "either to hold assemblies or to enter those places which they call their cemeteries." The edict was, of course, disobeyed, and Pope Sixtus II., with some of his deacons, was surprised and martyred in the Catacomb of Pretextatus. This Catacomb was situated in a vineyard on the opposite side of the road from the

Catacomb of St. Callixtus, and perhaps it had been selected as the place of meeting because it was less known to the public than that chief of Christian cemeteries. The secret, however, had been betrayed, and (as we learn from an inscription by Pope Damasus) the Holy Pontiff was apprehended whilst in the midst of a religious function. The faithful who were present vied with one another in offering themselves to martyrdom, in his company at least, if not in his stead, but only the deacons obtained the coveted privilege. The Bishop himself was led before the tribunal, condemned, and then brought back to the scene of his "crime," where he received the crown of martyrdom either in his pontifical chair itself, or at least so near to it that it was sprinkled by his blood. The charge on which he was condemned was distinctly this, "that he had set at nought the commands of Valerian." But in the following year these commands were revoked, and during the next fifty or sixty years the Catacombs come before us in successive periods of Church history as enjoying good or evil fortune according to the varying fortunes of the Church herself, of which they became a chief battlefield. If Valerian interdicted them, Gallienus, his son, restored them; and thus they were tolerated and forbidden, forbidden and tolerated again, according to the will of the Government, until at last, before the end of the century, they were confiscated altogether.

More than two centuries had now elapsed since the Catacombs were begun, and they had attained a degree of development far beyond anything that could have been anticipated. Divers modifications also had been gradually introduced in the execution of the work, and of these it will be worth while to give some account. We will take the cemetery of St. Callixtus as a specimen; for although in almost every Catacomb there is some difference in detail from the rest, caused either by some local peculiarity, or by the mere taste or caprice of those who made it, yet, in outline at least, the process of development must have been the same in all. It seems to have been something of this kind. At first a plot of ground in some suitable situation was either given by its Christian proprietor, or acquired by purchase, and secured by all necessary legal formalities—probably also enclosed by a wall or other fence—as a place of burial. A plan of excavation was then determined upon, and the work begun. Whilst as yet the *fossors* had had no experience of the consistency of the material in which they were to labour, and whilst they imagined themselves to be providing for the burial only of a few, they would naturally work freely and without much regard to economy of space. But as time went on the necessity for economy would become apparent; then they had recourse to various devices for securing it. They lowered the floors both of the vaults and galleries, so that they might receive more tiers of graves. They made the galleries somewhat narrower than before, and closer to one another. At the angles of their intersection, where the friability of the rock would not admit of full-sized graves being cut, they made smaller graves for infants, that the space might not be wasted. They did the same also even in the shelves of rock which had been left as a necessary support between the several tiers of graves. Everywhere unnecessary labour was spared; no more soil was removed than was absolutely necessary for the purpose required. The graves were made wider at the head and shoulders, and narrower at the feet; and if two bodies were to be buried in a double grave (*locus bisomus*), the soil was excavated only in exact proportion, the feet of the one being generally laid by the head of the other.

These expedients, however, could not materially enlarge the space available for graves, and the *fossors* were driven to excavate another flat (so to speak) either above or below the first. And here they were enabled more easily to provide chambers in which the faithful could assemble in time of persecution. The first subterranean chambers had been made small and plain, and rectangular in shape—mere family vaults apparently; but in the second and third floors we find them both more numerous, more spacious, and in a greater variety of forms, furnished also with *luminaria*, or shafts communicating with the surface of the ground, whereby light and air could be supplied to those who were assembled below. Some of them were decorated with cornices, columns, pilasters, brackets and chairs, hewn out of the solid rock. To the period of persecution belong also those galleries which connect parts of the more important cemeteries with the sandpits in their immediate neighbourhood—connections which were both studiously concealed, and, in some instances at least, designedly rendered dangerous to the use of strangers.

Other features in the development of the architecture of the Catacombs must be passed over, as they

Diogenes the Fossor.

cannot be appreciated except by means of a personal examination on the spot, or with the aid of more abundant plans and drawings than our present limits will allow. We must not, however, omit to say a few words about the noble band of workmen by whom these stupendous excavations were being made. We learn something about them even from the Catacombs themselves. Here and there, among the decorations of some of the vaults, may be seen the figures of men armed with pickaxes and lamps, and other instruments necessary for subterranean excavation, and several epitaphs have preserved to us the official title of these men: they were called *fossores*, or diggers. Their work must have been extremely laborious, and hence, in the imperial laws of the fourth and fifth centuries, they appear under a name derived from this circumstance. They are there called *copiatæ*, or labourers *par excellence;* but in all the inscriptions hitherto discovered in the Catacombs, they never have any other name than *fossores*, or *fossarii*. Their life must also have been one of continual danger and self-sacrifice. It was no mere venal service which they rendered to the Church, but a work of real devotedness. Moreover, they were necessarily in the confidence of the Church's rulers; they knew the exact place of burial of each martyr and confessor, the times and places appointed for the celebration of the holy mysteries, and so forth. We are not surprised, therefore, to hear, on the authority of St. Jerome, that they were reckoned among the *clerics;* and although they are not mentioned in the list of the Roman clergy sent to St. Cyprian about A.D. 240, we find them enumerated in an official document of the first decade of the fourth century, where they follow immediately after the bishop, priests, deacons, and sub-deacons. In the list furnished to St. Cyprian, it is probable that they are included among the *ostiarii*, with whose duties their own must have been in part identical as long as the Christians continued to worship in the Catacombs. However, be this as it may, there can be no doubt that during the earliest ages of the Church the *fossors* were supported, like the rest of her ministers, by the voluntary gifts of the faithful; and the whole work of the Catacombs was carried on by means of the mutual spontaneous liberality of the whole body of Christians, not by any fixed tax exacted for each grave that was required.

We have now completed our sketch of the outward history of the Catacombs during the ages of persecution. We have noted the vicissitudes of their fortunes at various times, traced the gradual process of their architectural development, and paid our tribute of admiration to the men who made them. Would that it were also possible to add a faithful abstract of the chronicles of these venerable sanctuaries during those eventful years! Many must have been the tender and stirring scenes of which they were the witnesses; but, alas! of most of these all written memorial has perished. Even of those which have reached us, the narrative has generally been corrupted by later embellishments, so that there are very few which rest on sufficiently authentic evidence to justify their introduction in this place. The following, however, are exceptions to this remark, and are too precious to be omitted.

Our first story belongs to the Pontificate of St. Stephen, and therefore to the year 256 or thereabouts. We gather it partly from the Acts of the Martyrs, and partly from the inscriptions which were set up at their tombs before those Acts were written, or certainly before that particular edition of the Acts was written which alone is now extant. The incidents of the story are these:—A wealthy Greek family, consisting of a gentleman and his wife and two children, and his brother, set sail for Italy. They were overtaken in their voyage by a storm, during which they made a vow to Pluto, and finally they reached their destination in safety. During their stay in Rome the brother (Hippolytus) renounced idolatry, and became a convert to the Christian faith, whereupon he devoted himself to the laborious and heroic work of a *fossor*. This probably happened during an interval when the Catacombs were under the ban of the Government, for we read that the scene of his labours was an *arenarium* or sandpit, and that he lived as well as worked in it. Certainly, the conditions of life would have been much more tolerable in a sandpit than in a proper Catacomb; and we have seen that, during times of persecution, a connection was often made between the cemeteries and any adjacent sandpit, in order to facilitate the means of entrance and of exit for the poor hunted Christians. The fact of

Hippolytus leading a solitary life in the sandpit is mentioned as though it were a singularity, as, indeed, we should have expected it to be ; and it is added, that his niece and nephew, aged nine and thirteen, used to visit and bring him food there, until at length, at the suggestion of Stephen, Hippolytus detained them one day, and so drew their parents to seek them in his hiding-place, where they were eventually converted by means of a miracle which they witnessed. Then, after being duly instructed and baptized, they distributed their wealth to the poor ; and having all received the crown of martyrdom, they were buried in the same *arenarium* in which they had been wont to assemble during life. It was the *arenarium* connected with the third story of the Catacomb of St. Callixtus, to which a grand staircase was once made straight down from the surface of the soil, for the convenience of the numerous pilgrims who came to do honour to Hippolytus, Adrias and Paulina, Neo and Maria. The staircase has been rediscovered, but the extremely friable nature of the soil has hitherto baffled every attempt thoroughly to explore the sandpit.

It has been already told how this Catacomb of St. Callixtus was, as it were, consecrated by the blood of St. Sixtus II., St. Stephen's successor. About thirty years later, during the Pontificate of St. Caius, who himself had to lie hid in a catacomb for several years, we read of a number of the faithful who were seen entering a cemetery on the Via Salara to visit the tombs of SS. Chrysanthus and Daria ; how, by order of the Emperor (Numerian), the entrance was at once closed, and a vast mound of sand and stones heaped up in front, that so they might all be buried alive, even as the martyrs they had come to venerate. St. Gregory of Tours tells us, that when the tombs of these martyrs were rediscovered after the ages of persecution had ceased, there were found with them, not only the relics of those worshippers who had been thus cruelly put to death—skeletons of men, women, and children lying on the floor—but also the silver cruets which they had taken down with them for the celebration of the sacred mysteries ; and De Rossi holds out hopes that some traces of this precious sanctuary may be restored even to our own generation. For we know that Pope Damasus (by whom it was discovered) abstained from making any of those changes whereby he sometimes decorated the martyrs' tombs, but contented himself with setting up an historical inscription, and opening a window in the adjacent wall or rock, that all might see, without disturbing, a monument so unique and touching ; and this was still visible in St. Gregory's days in the sixth century.

It is from another inscription of Pope Damasus that we learn the history of the noble young acolyte and martyr, St. Tharsicius, who was seized one day as he was leaving a catacomb in which the holy mysteries had just been celebrated, and was carrying the Blessed Sacrament secretly about his person to convey to some of the absent faithful, who were either sick, or had not dared to fly in the face of the law prohibiting the Christian assemblies. The youth sacrificed his life rather than betray to Pagan eyes the priceless treasure that had been intrusted to his keeping. Then they rifled his corpse, yet their profane curiosity was not gratified; and the holy martyr was buried in the cemetery of St. Callixtus, whence he had probably set out.

St. Agnes also belongs to the same period which we are trying to illustrate, but she belongs to its very last stage, during the persecution of Diocletian, when, as we have said, the Catacombs were altogether confiscated. Still this did not succeed in rigorously excluding the faithful. We know, from the irrefragable testimony of dated inscriptions, that even at such times as these the Christians managed to gain admission and to bury there. There is nothing, therefore, strange or inconsistent with history in the story of her parents having been engaged in prayer at her tomb two days after her martyrdom, when they were consoled by the vision of her glory in heaven; nor in that other story that her foster-sister, St. Emerentiana, was in the same place baptized in her own blood.

CHAPTER III.

THEIR HISTORY FROM A.D. 310 TO A.D. 850.

THE persecution of Diocletian ended in 306, but it was not until 311 that the Catacombs were restored to their natural owners and protectors, the Bishops of Rome. In that year the Pope Melchiades sent, by the hands of some of his deacons, letters from the Emperor Maxentius to the Prefect of the city, that he might recover legal possession of all "the ecclesiastical places" of which the Christians had been plundered; and amongst these places, the cemeteries were the most precious. About this time, if not earlier, other cemeteries also were made, more easily and at less cost, above ground instead of below; and during the next hundred years both places of burial were in use. If we may take the dated inscriptions as a guide in estimating the relative proportions in which they were used, we should say that burial in the Catacombs remained in the greatest favour until the latter half of the century. From the year 364 to the end, the balance is considerably on the other side; only one-third of the burials appear to have been in the subterranean cemeteries, and two-thirds above ground. Then from the year 400 to 410, burial in the Catacombs became more and more rare, until in that year it ceased altogether.

The portions of the Catacombs that were excavated during the fourth century vary considerably in character. In some parts, everything is on an exceptional scale of grandeur; the chambers are not only double, one on either side of the gallery, but even treble and quadruple, and of magnificent proportions. In other parts, on the contrary, there is nothing but a number of miserable galleries, executed with great economy, and destitute of all ornament; evidently they were required to meet the increasing wants of a large Christian population. It is during this same period that we meet with inscriptions recording contracts for the purchase of graves, and many more which, without entering into details, merely declare that the deceased had provided during his lifetime a place of burial for himself alone, or for himself and his wife, and perhaps some other relatives also. These have very rarely been found in the more ancient parts of the Catacombs. Indeed, such purchases would have proved a fruitful source of embarrassment in the days of persecution, when the *fossors* often used galleries whose walls had been already filled with graves as a convenient place in which to deposit the soil removed from the new galleries they were excavating, and sometimes even buried corpses in the pathways which they had thus filled. But this could not have been done if it had been necessary to reserve particular spots as the private property of persons hereafter to be buried there.

In the earliest of the inscriptions which record the purchase of graves, the *fossors* appear as the vendors; indeed, towards the end of the fourth century, it would almost seem as though the whole administration of the Catacombs had fallen into their hands. Each *fossor* now worked either independently, or with a partner if he preferred it; at least, the purchase is generally stated to have been made from one *fossor*, occasionally from two; and if the names of others of the same class are added, it is only to say that they assisted as witnesses of the contract. Once we even find the family of a *fossor* selling the graves which their father had excavated. In several of the inscriptions the price is named, as well as the names of the contracting parties; and some authors have attempted to estimate from these examples the ordinary cost of a grave in the Catacombs. Their calculations, however, cannot be accepted, for several reasons. First, the recorded prices are, in every instance, out of all proportion with the labour really expended on the grave; and secondly, they vary immensely, yet not according to any fixed principle. It seems safer, therefore, to conclude, with De Rossi, that the price was in each case proportionate to the means and good-will of the purchaser, that so provision might be made for the gratuitous burial of the poor out of the superabundant payments of the wealthy.

Another and a more important change than any which has yet been mentioned came over the Catacombs during the fourth century. It has been already mentioned that the devotion of the faithful naturally led them to look on the tombs of the martyrs with feelings of the most tender and pious affection; they desired, therefore, to manifest their love by some outward tokens—to exchange the primitive simplicity of their humble graves for something more suitable to their own altered condition. From the first moment, then, that it was possible, even in the very age of Constantine, grand basilicas were built over the tombs of the more celebrated saints, St. Peter, St. Paul, St. Agnes, St. Sebastian, and others. In all these instances, they aimed at enclosing the tomb they desired to honour within the precincts of the church; indeed, this was, of course, the central point of devotion in the new building. But it was impossible to dig the foundations and build the walls of such vast edifices without a great destruction of subterranean graves and galleries throughout the whole neighbourhood. Probably there were always some who regretted this necessity, and who would have preferred to see these venerable monuments of primitive Christianity left in their original form. Certainly at the end of some fifty or sixty years, about the year 370, there sat in the chair of Peter one who seems to have entertained these feelings, and who devoted himself therefore with singular zeal and prudence to the work of their preservation.

Pope Damasus (for it is he of whom we are speaking) sought diligently for all the tombs of historical note that had been hidden in days of persecution and not yet recovered. He had no means, indeed, nor apparently any desire, to crown them with basilicas of royal grandeur such as Constantine had built; but he did what he could, and what he thought necessary, both for the avoidance of scandal and danger among the innumerable pilgrims who now flocked from all parts of the world to visit the tombs of the martyrs, and also to preserve their memory to future generations. First, therefore, he made new staircases and additional shafts to the upper world to admit more light and air; he blocked up certain passages, so as to check indiscriminate rambles in the subterranean labyrinth, and to guide the pilgrims perforce to those particular shrines where they wished to pay their homage. He strengthened the friable tufa walls of some of the galleries which needed support by means of arches of brick and stone work. He enlarged some of the chambers, and ornamented many more; sometimes encasing their walls from top to bottom with marble; sometimes—" not content with Parian marble," as Prudentius says—even using much solid silver for the ornamentation of very special shrines. Finally, he composed short sets of verses in honour of some of the heroes he desired to honour—verses in which he either relates some interesting circumstance of their history which would otherwise have been lost, or records the repairs or ornaments which had been his own work. These inscriptions have been of the utmost service in fixing the geography of the cemeteries, and so in reconstructing their history. They are all exquisitely engraved on marble, and set up at the spots to which they severally belong; engraved, too, invariably by the same hand, the hand of an accomplished artist, Furius Dionysius Filocalus, who devoted himself to this work out of special love, as it would seem, to the Pontiff whom he so ably served.

The devotion of Pope Damasus to the Catacombs was as intelligent as it was ardent. He longed, as he himself tells us, to be buried in them, in a chamber where many of his martyred predecessors and other saints already lay; but he respected too much the integrity of their tombs, and prepared his place of burial therefore elsewhere. He built a place for the purpose aboveground, in which himself, his mother, and sister, were all buried. It would have been a happy thing for Christian archæology if others had been equally scrupulous; but numerous epitaphs tell us of men and women who had secured for themselves by purchase the right of a grave "behind the saints" (*retro sanctos*) or "near" (*ad*) such and such a saint, *i.e.*, near his tomb; and many a subterranean chapel still testifies, by the destruction of its original decorations, to the frequent gratification of this natural desire. It is not improbable that Pope Damasus forbade its indulgence to others, as he certainly denied it to himself. Anyhow, there was a rapid decline in the number of those who were buried in any part of the Catacombs during the latter part of his Pontificate.

Then came the fatal year 410, the year in which Rome was taken by Alaric,—the year in which, as St. Jerome says, "the most beautiful light of the world was put out: the Roman Empire was decapitated, and, to sum up all in one word, in the destruction of one city the whole world perished." In this year, the use of the Catacombs as Christian cemeteries came to an end, and it was never again resumed. Here and there, at rare intervals, a few exceptions may be found, even down to the middle of the fifth century; but, speaking generally, it may be said that they now ceased to be places of burial, and were only henceforth places of pilgrimage.

In 557, much mischief was done in them by the Goths, attracted, perhaps, by some report of the Parian marble and solid silver of which Prudentius had written with such enthusiasm. The mischief was repaired in part by the generosity of the people, in part by the care of the Popes. Pope Vigilius (A.D. 550) restored some of the monumental inscriptions of Pope Damasus which had been broken. It must be acknowledged that his restorations were not very successful; but this was not through any fault of his. Those were days of continual alarm and violence, and literature and the fine arts do not flourish in such an atmosphere. The artists, therefore, whom Vigilius had at his command were not worthy successors of

Filocalus; they were both ignorant and unskilful. Sometimes they do not seem to have known the Latin words they had to reproduce, and, when they knew them, often they could not spell them. They committed many offences against the laws both of prosody and of orthography. Nevertheless, we owe the Pope a debt of gratitude for having done what he could, for he has preserved to us some valuable records which would otherwise have perished.

During the next two hundred years matters did not mend. We read of many ordinances by the Popes designed for the protection of the cemeteries and for the celebration of mass in them. But by and by, when the Lombards attacked Rome in 756, the work of ruin made fresh and rapid strides, and, in fact, was soon completed. These men were Arians, and they broke in and carried off some bodies of the saints to take them home to their own churches in the North of Italy; so that, immediately afterwards, Pope Paul I., finding himself quite unable effectually to protect so many cemeteries situated all round the city and so far from its walls, determined to bring the bodies of the martyrs for safer custody into churches within the city. This work of translation, as it was called, though not continued by either of his immediate successors, was resumed by Pope Paschal I. in 817, and carried on by others, the latest instance on record belonging to the days of Leo IV. (A.D. 848). All these Popes assign as the cause for the translation the state of ruin to which the cemeteries were now reduced, and the horrible profanation to which they were continually exposed, parts of them being even used by farmers of the Campagna for the stabling of their sheep and oxen. From this time the real living history of the Catacombs was at an end. As in the beginning of the fifth century they had ceased to be used as places of burial, so in the first half of the ninth they ceased to be frequented for purposes of devotion. Henceforward there was nothing to keep them in the minds and hearts of men. They were neglected and then forgotten.

A few exceptions must be made to these remarks. To some cemeteries religious congregations of men or women had been attached from a very early date. These houses were established for the singing of the Divine praises day and night, in continuation of the primitive practice, when clergy and laity used to keep watch and sing psalms and hymns at the martyrs' tombs. As long as this was done, the adjoining cemeteries remained at least partially accessible, and were preserved from utter oblivion. This is why we read of occasional visits to the Catacombs of St. Agnes, St. Cyriaca, St. Sebastian, and one or two others, even during the eleventh and twelfth centuries. Numerous inscriptions, which the making of the modern *Campo Santo* in Rome has lately brought to light, demonstrate that there was a convent of nuns near San Lorenzo *fuori le mura*, as early as the fourth century. There had been another at the Basilica of St. Agnes since the days of Constantine;

and Pope Sixtus III. established a congregation of men at the Basilica of St. Sebastian on the Via Appia. This last has an interesting connection with our subject; for the cemetery at St. Sebastian's, which had been the temporary resting-place of the bodies of the Apostles Peter and Paul, was known as the Cemetery *ad Catacumbas*. How it came to be so called, or what is the meaning of the name, scholars are not agreed; neither would the settlement of the question add much to our knowledge of the Catacombs themselves, any more than if we could discover why another cemetery was called "The Cemetery at The Two Laurels" (*ad duas lauros*), and another, "The Cemetery at Cucumber Hill" (*ad divum cucumeris*). An accidental importance, however, attaches to the name of this particular cemetery, because it is now given also to all the other subterranean cemeteries of Rome, and even to the cemeteries of Naples, of Paris and Malta, of Sicily and Egypt, some of which have hardly any characteristics in common with them.

CHAPTER IV.

THEIR LOSS AND RECOVERY.

FROM the middle of the ninth century till nearly the end of the sixteenth, the Roman Catacombs had no history, and were practically unknown. At various times indeed during the fifteenth century, a few friars and strangers from Scotland, from Sicily, and the North of Italy, had somehow found their way into a corner of the Catacomb of St. Callixtus; and a few men of learning also, about the same time, visited both this and some other cemeteries. All these visitors have left their names inscribed upon the walls; but neither the friars nor the archæologists seem to have recognised the value of what they saw, nor taken pains to communicate their discovery to others. The whole subject lay in complete darkness, when, in the year 1578, an accidental circumstance brought it to light.

On the last day of May in that year, some labourers who were digging *pozzolana* in a vineyard on the Via Salara happened to break into a gallery of graves ornamented with Christian paintings, Greek and Latin inscriptions, and two or three sculptured sarcophagi. Such a discovery in an age of great intellectual activity naturally excited much curiosity, so that persons of all classes flocked to see it. "Rome was amazed," writes a cotemporary author, "at finding that she had other cities unknown to her concealed beneath her own suburbs, beginning now to understand what she had before only heard or read of;" "and in that day," says De Rossi, "was born the name and the knowledge of *Roma Sotterranea.*" Would that there had been born also at the same time, in the highest quarters of the Church, a sufficient appreciation of the importance of the discovery to have caused them to take it under their own immediate superintendence, and to pursue with care and diligence the researches to which it invited them. Had the ecclesiastical authorities of Rome adopted from the first some such means for the guardianship of the Catacombs and their contents as Pope Pius IX. in 1851, by intrusting them to a Commission of Sacred Archæology, or even as Clement IX. in 1688, by forbidding all excavations and removal of relics from them by private individuals, they would have been to us almost a Christian Pompeii—a true "city of the dead," yet exhibiting such abundant and authentic records of the first ages of the Roman Church as would have enabled us to form a very lifelike picture of our forefathers in the faith.

But alas! the work of destruction began almost as soon as it was discovered that there was anything to destroy; and the labours of the few who appreciated what had been found, and would fain have handed down to posterity an accurate account of it, could hardly keep pace with the destroyer. From the first there were a chosen few who laboured hard in this new field of Christian archæology—in particular, a Spanish Dominican friar and two young Flemish laymen; but the fruits of their labours were never given to the public; and when Bosio took the work in hand, only fifteen years after the date of the original discovery, the paintings in the crypts on the Via Salara had already been destroyed.

Bosio seems to have paid his first visit to the Catacombs, in company with the learned antiquarian Pompeo Ugonio and some others, on the 10th of December 1593. They penetrated into a catacomb about a mile distant from St. Sebastian's, and having found their way to a lower level by means of an opening in the floor of one of the chapels, they incautiously proceeded so far, that when they wished to return they could not recognise the path by which they had come. To add to their perplexity and alarm, their lights failed them, for they had remained underground much longer than they had intended, and "I began to fear," he says, "that I should defile by my vile corpse the sepulchres of the martyrs." However, this accident did not damp his courage nor divert him from his purpose; he only took precautions against its recurrence, and then devoted himself for the remaining thirty-six years of his life to the thorough prosecution of the work he had begun. He gave himself up with untiring energy to researches in the bowels of the earth on the one hand, and among old books and manuscripts on the other. His industry in both was amazing. As to his literary labours, there are still extant some thousands of folio pages in his own handwriting, showing with what care he had read the Fathers, Greek, Latin, and Oriental; the collections of canons and councils, ecclesiastical histories, lives of the saints, and an immense number of theological treatises, including those of the schoolmen; in fact, every work within his reach in which he thought there was a chance of finding anything in illustration of his subject. He had also transcribed numerous Acts of the Martyrs, especially of those who had suffered in Rome, together with any other ancient records which promised to throw light upon the topography of the Christian cemeteries. And when he had learnt in this way something as to the probable position of a catacomb, then began the anxious, fatiguing, and even dangerous work of his subterranean researches. He would examine with the utmost diligence all the neighbouring fields and vineyards, in order to discover, if possible, some entrance by which he could penetrate; and often, after returning again and again to the same spot, his labour still remained unrewarded. At another time he would hear of some opening having been accidentally made into a catacomb, by the digging of a new cellar or a well; and on hastening to the spot, he would find perhaps that the whole place was so buried in ruins that ingress was impossible. Even when an entrance was once effected, he still had to force a passage, often by the labour of his own hands, through the accumulated rubbish of ages; for we must not suppose that the pioneers in the work of exploring the Catacombs after their rediscovery found the galleries clear and empty as they are seen by ordinary visitors at the present day; on the contrary, some were filled to the very roof with soil that had been washed down in the course of so many ages through the open *luminaria;* others had been the scene of wilful injury done by Goth or Lombard, or by neighbours nearer home seeking forbidden treasures, or only anxious to make use of caves and cellars which they found ready-made to their hands. In some places the roofs of the galleries and chambers had given way under the shock of earthquakes, or from the continual disturbance of the surface of the ground for the purposes of building or agriculture. In a word, the work of exploration was attended with very real danger, so that no Christian archæologist can ever speak of Antonio Bosio—the Columbus, as he is often and deservedly called, of this new world of subterranean Rome—without admiration and enthusiasm.

He was preparing to communicate to the world the fruits of all his toil, when he was cut off by death at the early age of fifty-four. His work, however, was published by others some five or six years later, in 1635. It was presently translated into German and Latin; an abridgment of it also was published in Holland, and at once the Catacombs resumed their ancient place as one of the wonderful sights of Rome which all intelligent travellers should visit. More visitors, however, were attracted by religious than by scientific motives, for Bosio's book had been the means of recalling some to the Catholic faith; and it was obvious that a voice, issuing as it were from the graves of some of the very earliest professors of Christianity, had a right to claim a hearing amid the din of religious strife which was then raging. Moreover, the devotion of the faithful had been excited by the hope of finding the bodies of saints and martyrs still lying in their graves; and concessions were therefore made to certain religious communities, and even to pious individuals, to search for them. In this way excavations were going on in a number of places at once, quite independently of one another, and no trustworthy record was kept of any. At last, in 1688, all private concessions were finally revoked, and henceforward the matter was reserved entirely to official hands. Even so, however, the scientific history of the Catacombs scarcely fared better than before. The literature which appeared on the subject, with hardly an exception, was controversial or apologetic rather than archæological. Nobody followed the historical and topographical system of Bosio; so that from his death down to the year 1740 we have no chronicles of each new discovery as it was made, but only a number of independent treatises, on single epitaphs perhaps, or on some special class of ancient monuments, out of which a diligent reader may laboriously extract for himself some very imperfect account of the results of the excavations that were in progress. Then there followed another hundred years, during the greater part of which the Catacombs remained almost in the same obscurity in which they had been buried for so many ages before Bosio was born.

At the beginning of the present century, tokens of a reviving interest in them may be traced in the proceedings of the Roman Archæological Society. But it was not until the year 1840 that this interest spread to any wide circle. The main impulse to it was then given by Father Marchi, S.J., who had been appointed *custode* of the Catacombs, and devoted himself to their study. In 1841 he began to publish a work on the monuments of early Christian art. Only the first volume, however—on architecture—was ever published, and then it was abandoned, partly in consequence of the political troubles of the times, by which his own Order was so seriously affected, but chiefly because, through the new discoveries that were made, he became conscious of its grave imperfections. He saw that he had begun to publish prematurely. He had, however, imparted his own enthusiasm to one of his scholars, who was at first the frequent companion of his subterranean exploring expeditions, whom he soon recognised as a valuable fellow-labourer, and whom he finally urged in the most pressing manner to undertake the work which he found too great for his own failing strength. This scholar was Giovanni Battista de Rossi, a Roman gentleman of good family, who has now for more than thirty years devoted his means, time, and talents to the prosecution of the task intrusted to him.

It has been well said that "archæology, as tempered and directed by the philosophic spirit, and quickened with the life and energy of the nineteenth century, is a very different pursuit from the archæology of our forefathers, and has as little relation to their antiquarianism as modern chemistry and modern astronomy have to their former prototypes, alchemy and astrology;" and nowhere can the justice of this remark be more keenly appreciated than in comparing De Rossi's works on the Catacombs with all that have gone before them. It is true that he has had some advantages which his predecessors had not; he has had access to newly recovered, or more carefully edited, documents, amongst which are even ancient guides to those sanctuaries, or at least exact descriptions of them, before they had been abandoned and their sacred treasures removed. He has also had the assistance, as intelligent as it has been indefatigable, of a brother whose mechanical genius has invented an instrument whereby the process of surveying and mapping any subterranean excavations has been rendered infinitely more easy, as well as more accurate, than it was before. But, after all, the chief secret of De Rossi's wonderful success is to be sought for rather in his own patient industry, his scrupulous caution, and the excellence of his scientific method, than in any extraordinary superiority of his literary or physical apparatus. He has studied every monument in its own place. He has examined with his own eyes every detail of the subterranean topography where it has been possible to penetrate, and then recorded his observations with a minuteness of analysis which it is sometimes almost wearying to follow in print, and which nothing but the most enthusiastic love of truth and the most indomitable perseverance could have enabled him to execute in fact. Thus his conclusions are drawn from the monuments themselves; or rather, they are little more than a *résumé* of the observations he has had to record upon those monuments. He has had before him, and, as far as possible, he sets before his readers, the precise situation and the measurements of all the crypts and galleries on all the different levels, and even of the thousands upon thousands of the individual tombs throughout this Christian necropolis; he marks the place and characteristics of every inscription, painting, and other monument he comes across in them; then, side by side with this immense mass of *data*, so important and so entirely trustworthy, he places every shred of old historical documents that he knows of, and which he thinks capable of throwing any light upon them; and finally proceeds to interpret them according to the very best rules of archæological criticism. The result has been a reconstruction of the history of the Catacombs, and in part also of their geography, in such perfect accord with all the facts and phenomena of the case, that there is probably no group of ancient monuments which can now be classified more exactly and with greater certainty than those in the Roman Catacombs.

CHAPTER V.

THEIR PAINTINGS AND SCULPTURE.

THERE is no branch of Christian archæology in which the labours of De Rossi have produced a more startling revolution than in the history of Christian art. When the Reformers of the sixteenth century protested against the use of pictures and images in churches, and boldly declared that it was contrary to the practice of primitive ages, Catholics had no monuments to appeal to in refutation of such a statement. The remains of the Christian literature of those times were scanty, and more or less silent upon the subject, and the paintings in the Catacombs were buried in darkness. Even when they were brought to light, it was not easy at once to speak positively as to their chronology. By and by, in proportion as the Catacombs were more explored, and it became possible to compare the paintings of one cemetery with those of another, and all of them with the paintings of Pompeii, the baths of Titus, the tomb of the Nasones, and other newly-recovered Pagan monuments whose ages were known, Catholic writers began to assume a bolder tone, and to claim a greater antiquity for the Christian use of painting than they had done before. Still it was impossible to fix any dates with precision so long as men confined themselves to the examination of single monuments, illustrating them perhaps with great learning, but without reference to the place where each monument had been found, the circumstances under which it had been executed, its connection with the history of the period, and the internal and external development of the Christian community at the time and place to which it belonged.

Now the Roman Catacombs are a vast gallery of ancient Christian art. Single specimens, indeed, may exist elsewhere, and wherever they are found they deserve attentive examination; but it is obvious that the largest and most valuable collection in the world is to be found in subterranean Rome; and here, if anywhere, the subject may be thoroughly sifted and settled. It is to the minuteness of the topographical researches of De Rossi that we are indebted for the solid basis on which the earliest chapters of the history of Christian art can now be made to rest. His plan here, as well as in every other branch of his subject, has been simply to note all he sees; and then, when he has collected sufficient materials, to arrange and generalise, not according to any preconceived theory of classification, but absolutely according to the strict, stern facts before him. If these facts, arranged in their true historical and geographical order, present a harmonious whole, and suggest or support a theory which can otherwise be shown to be probable, he accepts it gladly; if not, he is content to leave the facts to speak for themselves, and to trust to further discoveries, or to the ingenuity of future commentators, to introduce light and order where at present there may seem to be chaos. For he never shrinks from acknowledging his inability to explain this or that phenomenon, and he prefers to leave a matter in doubt rather than to dogmatise on insufficient authority. Such moderation naturally inspires confidence; and perhaps another presumption in favour of the impartial accuracy of his statements may be found in the fact that sometimes they militate against the theories of those who would assign to every monument a greater antiquity than it is entitled to, and sometimes against the theories of the opposite and more numerous school. On the whole, however, whatever his opinion may be as to the age of any particular monument that has been called in question, his testimony as to the free use of painting by the early Christians is distinct and positive, and supported by irrefragable proofs.

"It may be asked," he says, "whether it is credible that the faithful, in the age of the Apostles or their disciples, when the Church, fresh from the bosom of the image-hating synagogue, was in deadly conflict with idolatry, should have so promptly and so generally adopted and (so to speak) baptized the fine arts?" And he replies, "I can only say that the universal use of pictures throughout the subterranean cemeteries, and the richness, the variety, and the freedom of the more ancient types, when contrasted with the cycle of painting which I see becoming more stiff in manner and poorer in conception towards the end of the third century,—these things demonstrate the impossibility of accepting the hypothesis of those who affirm that the use of pictures was introduced little by little, on the sly, as it were, and in opposition to the practice of the primitive Church." He points out also that the (comparatively) flourishing condition of the fine arts, and the large number of their professors in Rome during the reigns of Trajan, of Hadrian, and of the Antonines, materially favoured the early introduction and development of pictorial art amongst the faithful; and that the conversion to Christianity of wealthy personages, and even of members of the imperial family, such as Domitilla and Flavius Clemens, told powerfully in the same direction; "whereas, on the contrary, the decline of the fine arts in the third and fourth centuries, the increasing cost of the handiwork of the painter and sculptor as their numbers diminished every day, the gradual but continuous impoverishment of public and private fortunes, which induced even the Senate and the Emperors to make their new monuments at the expense of others more ancient,—all this could not facilitate the multiplication of new works of Christian art during that period; so that, even if the faithful were gaining in the number of converts, in power and in liberty, they lost quite as much, if I may say so, in the conditions required for the flourishing of Christian art."

The reader will have observed that De Rossi insists in these passages upon the superiority of the Christian paintings of the first two centuries over those of the third and fourth; it does not enter into his argument in this place to speak of paintings executed at any later period, when the Catacombs had ceased to be used as burial-places, and were visited only from motives of piety. Neither does it form any part of our own plan to examine these later paintings at any length. We only mention here that, of course, there are such paintings, as it was not to be expected that the Christians would cease to decorate the places in which the relics of the martyrs still lay; but they are few in number as compared with the great mass of paintings throughout the Catacombs, and they are also so totally unlike those of the præ-Constantinian era, that it would be impossible for any intelligent person to mistake the one for the other. For the present, let us proceed to look more closely into the paintings of the earlier period.

Pliny tells us that in the days of Vespasian, *i.e.*, in the first century of the Christian era, the art of painting was falling into decay in Rome—that it no longer executed any great and original works, but was well nigh confined to the decoration of apartments. Now, this is precisely the branch of art for which there was the greatest demand—one might almost say, the only opportunity—in the Catacombs. What kind of chamber-decoration, then, was in fashion in Pagan houses and tombs (for the Pagans also used to decorate their tombs) about this time? There are not wanting numerous specimens, both in Pompeii and in the neighbourhood of Rome itself, from which to form an opinion. But in the absence of any copies of them here, let us read the general description of them given by a competent and impartial critic. Müller (in his work on "Ancient Art and its Remains"), after endorsing Pliny's judgment, which has just been quoted, goes on to say that "even in its degenerate state the art exhibited inexhaustible invention and productiveness. The spaces on the walls," he says, "are divided and disposed in a tasteful way; then into these spaces are introduced arabesques of admirable richness of fancy; the roofs are often in the form of arbours hung with garlands, interspersed with fluttering winged forms, and all this in lively colours, clearly and agreeably arranged and executed." Any one who is familiar with the Catacombs knows that this is exactly what is to be seen there over and over again, and that in those cemeteries to which we are induced *for other reasons* to assign the highest antiquity, we find all these things in the highest degree of perfection, and with the least admixture of anything distinctively Christian. This is so true, that a Protestant controversialist has even ventured to say that, on entering some of the most ancient chambers of the Catacombs, we hesitate for a moment as to the Pagan or Christian character of what we see. There is the same geometrical division of the roof, the same graceful arabesques, the birds

Painting on roof of most ancient part of Cemetery of St. Domitilla.

and flowers, just as Müller describes them; and it is only when we recognise a figure of the Good Shepherd, or Daniel in the lions' den, or some similar subject, occupying the central compartment of the whole, that our doubts are dissipated.

Look for a moment at the most graceful specimen of decoration on the last page; it is one of the most ancient in the Catacombs, and it comes from that one of which we saw in a former chapter the public entrance close to the high road, and which we said belonged to the noble Flavian family at the end of the first century. The whole roof of the vaulted passage is covered with the vine, trailing with all the freedom of nature, and little winged genii are fluttering among the leaves. Certainly we might suspect this of being Pagan, were it not that Daniel in the lions' den, Noe in the ark, and other undoubtedly Christian subjects, are close at hand to disabuse us of the suspicion. Or look at the painting of another vault on the opposite page. This is more stiff than the former, because it was executed nearly a century later; still, there is nothing to declare its Christian character until the eye rests on the Good Shepherd, who appears below the principal part of the decoration.

We are not saying that the artists who executed these paintings had no Christian meaning in them; on the contrary, we believe that they had, and that the paintings really suggested that meaning to those who first saw them. For we know, on the authority of Tertullian, that "the whole revolving order of the seasons" (which are represented in the second painting) was considered by Christians to be "a witness of the resurrection of the dead." This, therefore, was probably the reason why they were painted here; and no Christian needs to be reminded that our Lord

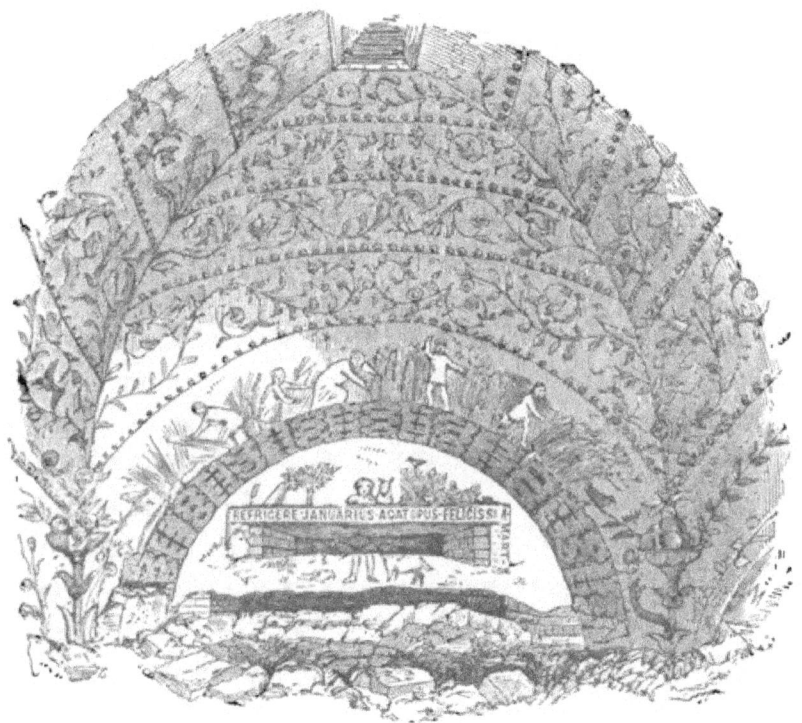

Painting on Vault of an Arcosolium in Cemetery of Prætextatus.

spoke of Himself under the image of a vine, which sufficiently explains the first painting. Still the fact remains that the representations themselves are such as might have been used by Christian and by Pagan artists indifferently. If any of our readers feel disappointed that the first essays of the Christian painter should not have had a more distinctly Christian character, they must remember that a new art cannot be created in a moment. If the Christian religion in its infancy was to make use of art at all, it had no choice but to appropriate to its own purposes the forms of ancient art, so far as they were pure and innocent; by degrees it would proceed to eliminate what was unmeaning, and substitute something Christian.

Some writers have supposed that Christians used at first Pagan subjects as well as Pagan forms of ornamentation; and they point to the figure of Orpheus, which appears in three or four places of the Catacombs, and to that of Psyche also, which may be seen about as often. So insignificant a number of exceptions, however, would scarcely suffice to establish the general proposition, even if they were in themselves inexplicable. But, in truth, the figure of Orpheus has no right to be considered an exception at all, for he was taken by some of the early Fathers as a type of our Lord; and it was even believed by some of them, that, like the sybil, he had prophesied about Him. Clement of Alexandria calls our Lord the Divine enchanter of souls, with evident reference to the tale of Orpheus; and the same idea will have occurred to every classical scholar, as often as he has heard those words of the Psalmist which speak of the wicked as "refusing to hear the voice of the charmer, charm he never so wisely." When, then, we find Orpheus and his lyre, and the beasts enchanted by his song, figured on the walls or roofs of the Catacombs, we have a right to conclude that the artist intended a Christian interpretation to be given to his work; and a similar explanation may be given of any other subjects of heathen mythology which have gained admittance there.

If we were asked to name the subject which seems to have been used most frequently in the early decorations of the Catacombs, we should give the palm to the Good Shepherd; nor is this preference to be wondered at. Any one who has meditated upon the words in which our Blessed Lord took this title to Himself, will easily understand why the first Christians, living in the midst of heathen persecutors, should have delighted to keep so touching an image always before them. They scratched it, therefore, roughly on the tombstone as they laid some dear one in the grave; they carved it on their cups, especially on the sacred chalice; they engraved it on signet rings and wore it on their fingers; they placed it in the centre of the paintings with which they covered the ceiling of their subterranean chapels, or they gave it the chief place immediately over the altar. We meet with it everywhere, and everybody can recognise it.

There are, however, one or two peculiarities in its mode of treatment which require a word of explanation. The shepherd is generally represented as a young man lightly clad, with his tunic girt high about his loins, denoting thereby his unwearied activity; he is surrounded by sheep, or he carries one on his shoulders, bearing it home to the fold,—the most tender act of his office. And there is nothing in this but what we might naturally have expected. But he is also sometimes represented with a goat instead of a sheep upon his shoulders; and, in later paintings, he has the pastoral reed or tuneful pipe either hanging on the tree by his side or he is playing on it. Now this last particular has no place in the gospel parable, and the former seems directly opposed to it, since the goat is the accepted symbol of the wicked, the sheep only of the good. Hence these points have been taken up by some critics, either as tokens of thoughtless carelessness on the part of the Christian artists, or as proofs that their work, whether consciously or unconsciously, was merely copied from some Pagan original. Neither of these remarks appears to be just. The images of a shepherd in Pagan art, with scarcely a single exception, are of a very different kind; and the particular details objected to are not only capable of receiving a Christian interpretation, they even express consoling Christian truths. St. Gregory Nazianzen speaks of the anxious care of the shepherd as he sits on the hillside, filling the air with the soft notes of his pipe, calling together his scattered flock; and he observes that in like manner the spiritual pastor, desirous to recall souls to God, should follow the example of his Divine Master, and use his pipe more frequently than his staff. Then, as to the substitution of the goat for the sheep, it was probably intended as a distinct protest against the un-Christian severity of those heretics, who in very early times refused reconciliation to certain classes of penitent sinners.

Not many, however, of the most ancient Christian paintings are of the same simple and obvious character as the Good Shepherd. The leading feature which characterises most of them is this, that they suggest religious ideas or doctrines under the guise of artistic symbols or historic types. One doctrine specially prominent in them, and most appropriately taught in cemeteries, is that of the resurrection and the everlasting life of happiness which awaits the souls of the just after death. It is in this sense that we must understand not only the frequent repetitions of the stories of Jonas and of Lazarus—the type and the example of a resurrection—but also of Daniel in the lions' den, and the three children in the fiery furnace. These last, indeed, very probably had reference also to the persecution which the Christians were then suffering, and were intended to inspire courage and a confident expectation that God would deliver them, even as He had delivered His chosen servants of old ; but, as they are spoken of in very ancient Christian documents (*e.g.*, in the hymns of St. Ephrem and in the Apostolic Constitutions) as foreshadowing the future triumph of the body over death, whence these too had been in a manner delivered, we prefer, in obedience to these ancient guides, to assign this interpretation to them ; at any rate, it is certain that this interpretation cannot be excluded. Figures also of the deceased, with arms outstretched in prayer, sometimes accompanied by their names, or standing in the midst of a garden, or, again, figures of birds pecking at fruits and flowers, we understand as images of the soul still living after death, received into the garden of Paradise, and fed by immortal fruits.

Sometimes there may be a difference of opinion perhaps as to the correctness of this or that interpretation suggested for any particular symbolical painting; but the soundness of the principle of interpretation in itself cannot be called in question, nor will there often be any serious difficulty in its application, among those who study the subject with diligence and candour. The language, both of Holy Scripture and of the earliest Fathers, abounds in symbols, and it was only natural that the earliest specimens of Christian art should exhibit the same characteristic. More was meant by them than that which met at first the outward senses; without this clue to their meaning, the paintings are scarcely intelligible,—with it, all is plain and easy.

Take, for example, the figure of an anchor, so repeatedly represented on gravestones and other monuments of the Catacombs; so rarely, if indeed ever, to be found on Pagan monuments. What influenced the early Christians in the selection of such a figure? what meaning did they attach to it? This enquiry forces itself upon our minds, if we are intelligent students of Christian archæology, anxious to understand what we see: and if we are also prudent and on our guard against being led astray by mere fancy, we shall conduct the enquiry by the same laws and principles as we should apply to the interpretation of some perplexing riddle in heathen art. We should first examine the literature of the age and people to whom it was supposed to belong, and see if any light could be thrown upon it from that source. In the present instance, therefore, we turn to the sacred literature of the Christians, and we find there a passage which speaks of the duty of "holding fast the hope that is set before us, which hope we have as an anchor of the soul, sure and firm." We assume, then, provisionally, as a basis of further enquiry, that an anchor may perhaps have been used as an emblem of Christian hope. Continuing our search in the same sacred books, we find that there was a special connection in the Christian creed between hope and the condition of the dead. It is written that Christians are not sorrowful about those who die, "as others who have no hope." The conclusion is obvious, that a reference to hope is just one of those things which might not unreasonably be looked for on a Christian's grave-stone, since it was something on which they prided themselves as a point of difference between themselves and others. This greatly confirms our conjectural interpretation of the symbol, and we proceed with some confidence to apply it to every example of its use that we can meet with; for if it is the right key, it cannot fail to unlock all the problems that will come before us. In doing this, we are first struck by the fact that in several instances the very names of the deceased persons on whose epitaphs the anchor is engraved, themselves also meant the same thing. They were called *Spes, Elpis, Elpidius, Elpizusa;* all names coming from the Latin or Greek word for hope. Next, we observe that many of these anchors are so fashioned as to contain a hidden yet unmistakable representation of a cross; and, reflecting that the one only ground of a Christian's hope is the cross of

Tombstone from the very ancient Crypt of St. Lucina, now united with the Catacomb of St. Callixtus.

Christ, we hail this also as lending further support to our theory. Yet once more, we find many of the epitaphs contain the same idea, expressed in distinct words written in the ordinary alphabet and not in these hieroglyphics, so to call them,—we find *Spes in Deo, Spes in Deo Christo* &c. Finally, we often find the anchor united with one or more of several other symbols, to which, by a similar but independent process, we can assign a certain signification. We try, then, whether our rendering of the anchor as equivalent to "hope" will *make sense*, as a schoolboy would say who was trying to translate a piece of Greek or Latin into English, in all these other places; and if it does, we are satisfied that our interpretation can be no longer disputed. A false reading of a single symbol might chance to fit one monument, or two, or three; but to say that any false reading will fit hundreds of separate monuments, fit all equally well, and succeed in extracting a consistent meaning from each, is to assert what no sane man can believe.

Those who know the way in which the interpretation of the Egyptian hieroglyphics was first guessed at, and then triumphantly established against all gainsayers, by a similar process of reasoning, will not dispute the soundness of the argument by which the meaning of the anchor has been arrived at. We cannot attempt to vindicate our interpretation of all the other symbols used by Christian artists with the same minuteness of detail, neither is it necessary. All will accept the dove as a fitting symbol of the simplicity, the gentleness, purity, and innocence of a Christian soul gone to its rest, and a sheep as fitly representing a disciple of Christ.

Another emblem, the fish, requires more words of explanation, because it is capable of receiving a double meaning. At first sight, our thoughts at once recur to the words of our Blessed Lord to St. Peter and his brother, "Follow me, and I will make you fishers of men," and no doubt this will sufficiently explain many old Christian paintings or sculptures in which the fish appears. Taking this idea for our guide, we can understand why a man angling and catching a fish should find a place on the walls of a church, whether above ground or below. Such a representation in these sacred places was inspired by the same doctrinal teaching, and suggested the same ideas, as were present to the old Christian preachers when they spoke of men being caught by the bait of charity and the hook of preaching, and being drawn out of the bitter waters of this world, not to have their life taken from them, which is the fate that awaits the natural fish when it is caught, but that they may be made partakers of a new and heavenly life. This, however, will not enable us to decypher other symbolical paintings into which the fish enters, and which are found with equal frequency among the decorations of the Christian cemeteries. It is necessary that we should learn another, and, as it would seem, a still more common use of the fish. Just as the dove might stand for the Holy Ghost, and also for a soul sanctified by the Holy Ghost—just as the lamb or sheep might stand either for the Lamb of God, or for those who are "the people of His pasture and the sheep of His hand"—so the fish, too, was used not only to represent a Christian, but also, still more frequently perhaps, Christ Himself. To understand how this could be, we must study a little Greek, which may be easily apprehended, however, even by those who are not scholars, if they will fix their attention for a few moments on the accompanying plan :—

I ΗCOΥC = Jesus
X PICTOC = Christ
Θ EOΥ = of God
$Υ$ IOC = Son
C ΩTHP = Saviour

The Greek for fish is here written perpendicularly, one letter above another, $IX\Theta YC$; and it is seen that these five letters are the initial letters of five words, which, together, contain a tolerably complete account of what Christ is. He is JESUS CHRIST, SON OF GOD, SAVIOUR. Thus, this one word, $\iota\chi\theta\upsilon\varsigma$, or fish, read in this way, tells a great deal about our Lord's name and titles; it is almost a miniature creed, or, as one of the Fathers expresses it, "it contains in one name a whole multitude of holy names." It would take us too long to enquire into the origin of this device for expressing our Lord's name and titles in so compendious and secret a form. Clearly, whoever may have invented it, it was very ingenious, and specially convenient at those times and places where men dared not speak of Him freely and openly. We cannot say when it began, but it was in universal use throughout the Church during the first three hundred years of her life, and then, when she was in the enjoyment of peace and liberty, it gradually dropped, first out of sight in Christian monuments, and then out of mind also in Christian literature. But, during the ages of persecution, it had sunk deep into the habits of Christian thought and language; it became, as it were, a part of the very Catechism,— every baptized Christian seems to have been familiar with it, whether he lived on the banks of the Tiber or of the Po, of the Loire, of the Euphrates, or of the Nile. In all these parts of the world, writers in books, poets in hymns, preachers in sermons, artists in painting, the very masons themselves on gravestones, made use of it without a word of explanation, in a way that would utterly mystify any modern Christian community. Who would now dream of carving or painting a fish upon a gravestone in a Christian churchyard? yet scores of graves in the Catacombs were so marked, and some of them with hardly a word or an emblem upon them besides. Or what meaning could we attach to the picture of a dove or a lamb standing on a fish's back, if we did not understand that the fish represented Christ, and the dove or the lamb a Christian, so that the whole symbol stood for a Christian soul supported by Christ through the waves and storms of life? Or again, only imagine a Christian in these days having buried with him, or wearing round his neck during life, a little figure of a fish cut in ivory, or crystal, or mother of pearl, or some still more costly material? Yet a number of those who were buried in the Catacombs did this; and some of these fish even bear an inscription, calling upon the fish to be a Saviour!

It was necessary to give this explanation of certain symbols, and to justify it by sufficient examples, before we proceed to study any of the more complex paintings in the Catacombs. But now, with these thoughts in our minds, let us enter the Cemetery of St. Callixtus, and look on a figure represented two or three times on a wall of one of its most ancient chambers: a fish swimming and carrying on its back a basket of bread, and in the midst of the loaves of bread, a glass vessel containing a red liquid. What is this but bread and wine, the elements of the Sacrament of Love, and Jesus Christ Its reality? St. Jerome, when speaking of a holy bishop of Toulouse who had sold the gold and silver vessels of his church to relieve the poor, uses these words, "What can be more rich than a man who carries the body of Christ in a basket of wicker-work, and the blood of Christ in a vessel of glass?" Here are undeniably the basket of wicker-work and the vessel of glass; and who can doubt that we have the other also, veiled under the figure of the fish?

Let us go to another part of the same cemetery, and consider a painting which with some variations is repeated in three or four successive chambers, all opening out of one of the primitive galleries. Bread and fish lie on a three-legged table, and several baskets of bread are arranged along the floor in front of it, or a man and woman stand by the side of the table. The woman has her arms outstretched in the form of a cross, the ancient attitude of Christian

F

prayer; the man, too, is stretching forth his hands, but in another way: he holds them forward, and especially his right hand, over the bread and fish, in such a way as to press upon every Catholic intelligence the idea that he is blessing or consecrating what is before him. To modern eyes, indeed, his vestment does not look worthy of one engaged in the highest act of Christian worship; perhaps, at

Consecration of the Holy Eucharist.

first sight, it almost strikes us as hardly decent. Nevertheless, to the Christian archæologist, this very vestment is a strong confirmation of the view we are taking of the real sense of the painting. For it is the Greek *pallium*, or philosophers' cloak; and we know that at the time to which this painting belongs (the end of the second or beginning of the third century) it was a common practice to preach the Word of God in this particular costume. Tertullian, who was living at the same time, wrote a treatise *De Pallio*, in which, in his own peculiar style, he defended its use, and congratulated the *pallium* on its promotion to be a Christian vestment. It was not until fifty years later that St. Cyprian objected to it, both as not sufficiently modest in itself and as vainglorious in its signification.

If there were any lingering uncertainty as to whether these figures were really intended to have reference to the Holy Eucharist, or whether our interpretation of them may not have been fanciful and arbitrary, an examination of the other decorations of the same chambers will suffice to remove it. For it will be seen that, whilst in closest connection with them are other suitable emblems or figures of the same Divine Sacrament, they are also uniformly preceded by representations of the initiatory Sacrament of the Christian covenant, without which no man can be admitted to partake of the Eucharist; and they are followed by a figure of the Resurrection, which our Lord Himself most emphatically connected with the eating of His flesh and the drinking of His blood, saying, "He that eateth my flesh and drinketh my blood, hath everlasting life, and I will raise him up at the last day." These three subjects, Baptism, the Holy Eucharist, and the Resurrection occupy the three perfect sides of the chamber, the fourth side being, of course, broken by the entrance; and, taken in their right order, they faithfully depict the new life of a Christian; the life of divine grace, first imparted by baptism, then fed by the Holy Eucharist, and finally exchanged for an everlasting life of glory.

Let us look at the figures of these subjects in detail, and see how they are represented here. First, we have Moses striking the rock, a scene which occurs over and over again in the Catacombs, and which in these chambers commences the series of paintings we are examining; it is to be seen on the

The Smitten Rock.

left-hand wall as we enter. St. Paul tells us that "the rock was Christ;" the water, then, which flowed from it must be those streams of Divine grace whereby His disciples are refreshed and sustained during their pilgrimage through the wilderness of this world, and this grace is first given in the waters of baptism. Next we have a man fishing, which has been already explained; and (in one instance at least) this is followed by another man performing the very act of baptism on a youth who stands before him; the youth stands in the water, and the man is pouring water over his head. Lastly, on the same wall, is the paralytic carrying his bed on his shoulders—the same, doubtless, who was miraculously cured at the pool of

The Sacrament of Baptism.

Bethsaida, which pool the fathers of the Church uniformly interpret as typical of the healing waters of the Christian sacrament.

On the wall opposite the doorway, the central scene is a feast wherein seven men are seated at a

Eucharistic Feast.

table, partaking of fish and bread; and there is a history in the last chapter of St. John's Gospel, of which it may be taken as a literal representation. It was when our Lord "showed Himself to His disciples at the Sea of Tiberias, and He showed Himself, after this manner. There were together Simon Peter and Thomas who is called Didymus, and Nathanael who was of Cana of Galilee, and the sons of Zebedee, and two others of His disciples"—seven in all. "And they went a-fishing, but caught nothing. Jesus appeared to them on the shore." Then there follows the miraculous draught of fishes; and as soon as they came to land, they saw "hot coals lying, and a fish laid thereon, and bread. Jesus saith to them, Bring hither of the fishes which you have now caught. And Jesus cometh and taketh bread and giveth them, and fish in like manner." Such is the letter of the gospel narrative; but this narrative is in fact a mystical and prophetic representation of the Church gathered together out of the waters of the world, and fed by the Holy Eucharist. The hundred and fifty-three great fishes that were caught represent the large numbers of the faithful that were drawn into the Church by apostolic preaching; the fish laid on the hot coals is Jesus Christ in His Passion, His Body "delivered for us" on Mount Calvary, given to us also to be our food in the Blessed Sacrament whereby "we show the death of the Lord until He come." The faithful caught in the net of the Church must be brought to that broiled fish (*Piscis assus, Christus passus*, says St. Augustine), that crucified Lord, and they must be incorporated with Him by partaking of the living Bread which came down from Heaven.

Sacrifice of Isaac.

Such is the full meaning of the scene at the Sea of Tiberias, as interpreted according to the unanimous

Resurrection of Lazarus.

consent of the Fathers; and the adjuncts of this picture show that it was intended to be so understood here also; for on one side is the figure of the consecration already described; and on the other, the sacrifice of Isaac by his father, which was surely a most lively type of the sacrifice of Christ upon the altar; wherein blood is not really shed, but the Lamb is only "*as it were* slain," just as Isaac was not really slain, but was received back from the dead, "for a parable." Lastly, as has been mentioned before, there follows on the third wall of the same chamber the natural complement of the rest; the doctrine of the Resurrection, as contained in the fact of the rising again of Lazarus. Thus, this whole series of paintings, executed at the end of the second century, or within the first twenty or thirty years of the third, and repeated (as has been said) in several successive chambers, was a continual homily, as it were, set before the eyes of the faithful, in which they were reminded of the beginning, progress, and consummation of their new and supernatural life.

We do not say that every modern Christian who looks at these paintings will thus read their meaning at once; but we believe that all ancient Christians did so, because it is clear from the writings of the Apostles themselves and their successors, that nothing was more familiar to the Christian mind of those days than the symbolical and prophetical meaning of the facts both of the Old and of the New Testaments. They believed the facts themselves to have taken place just as they are recorded, but they believed also that they had a mysterious signification, whereby the truths of the Christian faith were insinuated or expressed, and that this was their highest and truest meaning. " Perhaps there is no one recorded miracle of our Lord," says St. Gregorgy, " which is not therefore selected for recording because it was the type of something to happen in the Church ; " and precisely the same was felt to be true also of the histories of the patriarchal and Jewish dispensations. " All these things had happened to them in figure, and they were written for our correction, upon whom the ends of the world are come."

It may not be often possible to trace as clearly as we have just done in a single instance, the logical order and dependence of the several subjects that were selected for representation in each chamber of the Catacombs ; they may not always have been so admirably arranged as to be in fact equivalent, as these were, to a well-ordered dogmatic discourse. Nevertheless it is only when read in this way, that the decoration of the Catacombs can be made thoroughly intelligible ; and it is certain that some such meaning must have been intended from the first. The extremely limited number of Biblical subjects selected for representation, while such an immense variety is really contained in the Bible (and so many of those that are neglected might have seemed equally suitable for the purpose), and then again, the thoroughly unhistorical way in which these few subjects are dealt with, shows clearly that the principle of selection was theological rather than artistic.

The artists were not left to indulge their own unfettered fancy, but worked under ecclesiastical supervision; and the Bible stories which they depicted were not represented according to their historical verity, because they were not intended to be a souvenir of past facts, but to symbolise and suggest something beyond themselves. In order, therefore, to understand them, it is necessary to bring them face to face with the Christian doctrines which they foreshadow.

Look, for example, at the numerous pictures of Noe in the ark which appear in the Catacombs, all resembling one another, but none resembling the reality. Instead of a vessel, three stories high, containing eight human beings and specimens of every kind of animal, we see only a narrow box, barely large enough to hold one person, and that person sometimes a lady, whose name is also inscribed upon it perhaps, being the same lady (as we learn from the inscription) who lies buried in the adjacent tomb. If all ancient Christian literature had perished, we should have been at a loss to comprehend this enigma; but as soon as we know that the Fathers of the Church speak of it as an acknowledged fact, which "nobody doubts" (to use St. Augustine's words), that the Church was typified by the ark, a

Noe in the Ark.

ray of light begins to dawn upon us; and when we call to mind that St. Peter himself speaks of the waters of baptism as saving men's souls, "even as Noe and his family were saved by the waters of the flood," all is at once made clear. We see plainly that the friends of the deceased have intended to signify that he had been received into the ark of the Church and made a Christian by baptism. And if they had added to the composition, as they often did, the figure of a dove bringing an olive branch to the person standing in the ark, this also enters into the same interpretation; it was symbolical of that Divine peace which comes to the soul in this world by faith, and which is a pledge of the peace given by everlasting happiness in the next.

The frequent repetition of the story of Jonas in a

Scenes from the History of Jonas.

Christian cemetery needs no explanation, our Lord himself having put it forward as a type of His own resurrection, and so a pledge of ours also. The particular form, however, under which this story appears, was not suggested, as Noe's ark was, by the place which it held in the cycle of Christian doctrine, but rather by a certain Pagan model with which the Romans of that day were very familiar. The mythological tale of Andromeda, and the sea-monster to which she was exposed on the coast near Joppa (for so the story ran), was a favourite subject for the decoration of the walls in Roman villas, temples, and other public buildings. It may be seen in Pompeii, and, much nearer to the Catacombs, in Rome itself— *e.g.*, in the barracks of one of the cohorts of the imperial police, discovered a few years ago in Trastevere; and in both places the monster is the precise counterpart of that which is always represented as swallowing or casting up Jonas; a kind of dragon, with large head and ears, a long slender neck, and a very tortuous body. Of course, in the infancy of Christian art, it was convenient to have a model at hand to represent an unknown monster, and, as we have said, we do not doubt that this is the true history of its origin. Still this was not the only reason which recommended the adoption of so grotesque a form; it offered the further advantage of creating as strong a contrast as possible between this "great fish," which was a type of death, and the ordinary fish, which, as we have seen, was the recognised symbol of the Author of life.

Another incident in the life of Jonas, which was often painted in the Catacombs, was his resting on the east side of the city of Nineve, under the shade of a certain plant which God caused to grow up for his protection, and which He again caused as suddenly to wither away. In the days of St. Jerome and St. Augustine there was a dispute between those learned doctors as to the precise nature of this plant; and in the course of it St. Jerome appealed to these paintings as bearing testimony in favour of his own rendering of the Hebrew word. We need not enter into the merits of the dispute, but it is important to note the fact of the appeal, as it peremptorily refutes the ridiculous assertions of certain authors of the present day, who would assign very recent dates to these and similar paintings in the Catacombs. We know that St. Jerome was very fond, when a boy, of visiting these places, and it is interesting to hear him appealing to the paintings he had seen in them as to "ancient witnesses." It would be still more interesting, if we could say with certainty what were the motives which led the ancient Christians to choose this subject for such frequent contemplation; whether they read in it only a very striking lesson as to the watchfulness of Divine Providence, or whether it had a more subtle meaning, as a type of the mercy of God which overshadows the souls of the faithful in the long sleep of death which goes before the Sun of the Resurrection. But where no clue is supplied by the writings of cotemporary, or nearly cotemporary authors, we prefer to keep silence rather than to insist on any doubtful interpretation. All that need be said is that such a painting was certainly not out of place in a Christian Church or cemetery, any more than the story of Adam and Eve, or any other

Biblical narrative which has reference to the doctrines or promises announced by Christianity to the world.

We do not pretend to enumerate here all the subjects from the Old and New Testaments that were painted in the Catacombs. We are but naming those that were used most frequently, that seem most interesting, or whose signification can be most precisely determined. Those who have seen the Catacombs themselves will call to mind others of which we have not spoken, but we think their meaning is generally obvious so as to need no explanation. We will name one class only of these paintings; those in which our Lord and His Blessed Mother appear. Our readers will hardly expect to find anything that pretends to be a portrait of either one or the other. We have seen that the disposition in primitive Christian art was to represent facts rather than persons, and the mystery which the facts signified rather than the facts themselves. Christ, therefore, appears most commonly in the typical character of the Good Shepherd, and as such is represented in appropriate form and with suitable accessories, or He sits in the midst of His Apostles, with a chest of volumes at His feet, as the Great Teacher of the world. Once, indeed, His head and bust form a medallion occupying the centre of a roof in a chamber of the Cemetery of St. Domitilla, the same in which appear Orpheus and his lyre. It is a work of the third century; there is more evidence of an intention to give a definite individual type of countenance, neither is the type altogether unlike that which the practice of later ages has consecrated by traditional usage. Nevertheless others of the fourth century are evidently not copies of the same model, so that it is clear that in those early days there was no uniform agreement upon the subject.

The B. Virgin and Isaias, from Cemetery of St. Priscilla.

Our Blessed Lady appears principally in the scene of the Adoration of the Magi. Two, three, or four of these men (according to the arrangement of the group and the space at the artist's disposal) stand in their Oriental dress, presenting their gifts to Christ who sits on Mary's knee. Once or twice also the

Holy Child appears in His Mother's arms, or before her breast, without reference apparently to any

The B. Virgin and Magi.

particular event in their lives, but either absolutely alone, or standing opposite to Isaias, as though presenting in themselves the fulfilment of his prophecies.

The B. Virgin, from the Cemetery on Via Nomentana.

One of these paintings in the Catacomb on the Via Nomentana belongs to the fourth century; but for another of far higher artistic merit, to be seen in the Catacomb of St. Priscilla, the most competent judges do not hesitate to claim almost apostolic antiquity; and the claim is supported by many and weighty arguments. We cannot, however, discuss them here, for we have already exceeded the limits we had proposed to ourselves.

In conclusion, we will give a slight sketch of the successive phases in the development of Christian art within the limits of the first three centuries; for, thanks to De Rossi's almost microscopic examination of every accessible corner of subterranean Rome, even this is now possible. As each of these phases was derived from its predecessor by a natural sequence of ideas, it is not pretended that they are separated from one another by strict chronological boundaries which are never transgressed; yet the characteristics of the several periods are, in the main, sufficiently distinct to allow of their being followed as safe guides in determining, at least approximately, the age of any particular class, or even individual specimen of ornamentation.

We have already seen that primitive Christian art sprung out of an alliance of ancient forms with new ideas; in its outward physiognomy it proceeded directly, in point of style and method of execution, from the school of Pagan decorative art, but it was animated by a new life; and therefore it began at once to create a pictorial cycle for itself, taken partly from historical and partly from allegorical materials.

G

At first the allegorical element greatly predominated. The fish and the anchor, the lamb and the dove, the shepherd and the fisherman, may be named as the most prominent examples; and all these during the first, or, as it has been styled, the hieroglyphic or ideographic period of Christian art, were characterised by the utmost simplicity. The principal figure usually stood alone; the fisherman is catching a fish, or the shepherd is carrying a sheep upon his shoulders, and nothing more.

In the second period—*i.e.*, from the middle of the second to the middle of the third century—the Good Shepherd occurs less frequently, and is represented less simply; he carries a goat, or he plays his pipe; he stands amid trees in a garden, or in the midst of his flock, and the several members of his flock stand in different attitudes towards him, marking a difference of internal disposition. Other figures also undergo similar changes; different emblems or different typical histories are blended together, and the result is more artistic; a more brilliant translation, so to speak, is thus given of the same thoughts and ideas with which we have been familiar in a more elementary form from the beginning. This change, or rather this growth, was in truth only the natural result of time and of the pious meditation of successive generations of Christians exercised upon the history of their faith and upon the outward representations of its mysteries, in which their forefathers had always delighted. The bud had expanded, and the full-blown flower displayed new beauties— beauties which had been there indeed before, but unseen. Thus we meet again with the apostolic fisherman, but the river in which he fishes is now a mystical river, formed by the waters which have flowed from the rock struck by Moses. More Bible histories are made use of; or, if not now introduced for the first time, are used more frequently—the history of Daniel and of Jonas, the sacrifice of Abraham, the resurrection of Lazarus, the healing of the paralytic at Bethsaida, and others. And as all these histories have been illustrated in the writings of cotemporary Fathers, the monuments which represent them are of the highest value as an historical expression of what Christians in those days believed and taught. Both the writings and the paintings are evidently the faithful echo of the same doctrinal teaching and tradition.

Then follows a third period in the history of Christian art, which, if the first two have been justly compared to its spring and summer, may itself be certainly called its autumn. It extends from the middle of the third century to the age of Constantine; and during this period there is a certain falling off of leaves, accompanied by a further development of the flower, without, however, any addition to its beauty. The symbolical element is sensibly diminished; what we have ventured to call Christian hieroglyphics are almost or quite abandoned; the parables also are less used, and even the historical types are represented in a more hard and literal form.

If Moses is still seen striking the mystical rock, the literal or historical Moses is at his side, taking off his shoes before drawing near to the burning bush; or the Jews are there, in their low round caps, drinking of the waters; or if it is desired to keep the mystical sense of the history before the people, it is

Glass from the Catacombs, now in Vatican Library.

deemed necessary to inscribe the name of PETRUS over the head of Moses, as we see in two or three specimens of the gilded glasses found in the Catacombs, and belonging probably to the fourth century. Christ no longer appears as the Good Shepherd, but sits or stands in the midst of His Apostles, or, still more frequently, miraculously multiplies the loaves and fishes. The fish is no longer the mystical monogram, "containing a multitude of mysteries," but appears only as a necessary feature in the representation of this same miracle. Lazarus appears swathed like a mummy, in accordance, as we know, with the fact; but earlier artists had idealised him, and made him rise from the tomb young, free, and active. The three children refusing to adore the image set up by Nabuchodonosor are brought forward, and placed in juxtaposition with the three wise men adoring the Infant Jesus, suggesting a comparison, or rather a contrast, very suitable to the altered circumstances of the times.

This last remark, however, must not be allowed to mislead us. We must not imagine that the chronological sketch which has been here attempted of the development of Christian art has been in any way suggested by a consideration of what was likely to have been its course in consequence of the history of the Christian society. The sketch is really the result of a very careful induction from the laborious researches which De Rossi has made into the chronology of the several parts of the Catacombs; and if there proves to be a correspondence between the successive variations of character in the works of art that are found there, and the natural progress of the Christian mind or the outward condition of the Christian Church, these are purely "undesigned coincidences," which may justly be urged in confirmation of our conclusion, though they formed no part of the premisses. We may venture also to add, that the conclusions were as contrary to the preconceived opinion of their discoverer as of the Christian world in general. Nothing but the overwhelming evidence of facts has forced their acceptance; but from these there is no escape. When it was found that the oldest *areæ* in the cemeteries are precisely those that are richest in paintings, and those in the best style, whereas in the more modern *areæ* the paintings are less in number, poorer in conception, and inferior in point of execution, it was impossible not to suspect the justice of the popular belief, that the infant Church, engaged in deadly conflict with idolatry, had rejected all use of the fine arts, and that it was only in a later and less prudent age that they had crept, as it were, unobservedly into her service; and as fresh and fresh evidence of the same kind has been multiplied in the course of the excavations, a complete revolution has at length been effected in public opinion on this matter. Even Protestant writers no longer deny that, from the very first, Christians ornamented their subterranean cemeteries with painting; only they insist that this was done, "not because it was congenial to the mind of Christianity so to illustrate the faith, but because it was the heathen custom so to honour the dead." If by this it is only meant that Christians, though renewed interiorly by the grace of baptism, yet continued, in everything where conscience was not directly engaged, to live conformably to the usages of their former life, and that to ornament the tombs of the dead had been one of those usages—it is, of course, quite true. Nevertheless it is plain from the history that has here been given, that the earliest essays of Christian art were much more concerned with illustrating the mysteries of the faith than with doing honour to the dead.

Our space will not allow, neither is it necessary, that we should enter at any length into the history of Christian sculpture, since the same general laws of growth presided over this as over painting. It must be remembered, however, that sculpture was used much more sparingly, and did not attain its full Christian development nearly so soon as the sister art. There was no room for it in the Catacombs except on the faces and sides of the sarcophagi, which were sometimes used there for the burial of the dead; neither was it possible to execute it with the same freedom as painting. The painter, buried in the bowels of the earth, prosecuted his labours in secret, and, therefore, in comparative security, without fear of any intrusion from the profane; but the work of the sculptor was necessarily more public; it could not even be conveyed from the city to the cemetery without the help of many hands, and it must always have run the risk of attracting a dangerous degree of general attention. We are not surprised, therefore, at hearing that some of those sarcophagi which are found in the most ancient parts of the Catacombs seem rather to have been purchased from Pagan workshops than executed by Christians; those, for instance, on which are figured scenes of pastoral life, of farming, of the vintage, or of the chase, genii, dolphins, or other subjects equally harmless. Sometimes it might almost seem as though the subjects had been suggested by a Christian, but their Christian character blurred in the execution by some Pagan hand, which added a doubtful or unmeaning accessory,

Sarcophagus still to be seen in the Cemetery of San Callisto.

Very ancient Sarcophagus, found in Crypt of St. Lucina.

—*e.g.*, a dog at the side of the shepherd. On some others there are real Pagan subjects, but these were either carefully defaced by the chisel, or covered up with plaster, or hidden from sight by being turned towards the wall.

When, however, in progress of time, all fear of

danger was past, the same series of sacred subjects as are seen in the fresco-paintings of the second and third centuries is reproduced in the marble monuments of the fourth and fifth; only they appear, of course, in their later, and not in their earlier form; often even in a still more developed and literally historical form than in any of the subterranean paintings. Thus Adam and Eve no longer stand alone, one on either side of the fatal tree, but the Three Persons of the Holy Trinity are introduced in the work of creation and the promise of redemption. Adam receives a wheat sheaf, in token that as a punishment for his sin he shall till the ground, and to Eve a lamb is presented, the spinning of whose wool is to be part of her labour. Daniel does not stand alone in the lions' den, but Habacuc is there also, bearing in his hand bread, and sometimes fish, for the prophet's sustenance. To the resurrection of Lazarus the figure of one of his sisters is added, kneeling at our Lord's feet, as though petitioning for the miracle. Our Lord stands between St. Peter and St. Paul, and He gives to one of them a volume, roll, or tablet, representing the new law of the Gospel. On the gilded glasses which belong to the same period the legend is added, *Lex Domini*, or *Dominus legem dat*. The Apostles are distinguished, the one as the Apostle of the Jews, the other of the Gentiles; and even two small temples or churches are added, out of which sheep are coming forth; and over one is written Jerusalem, and over the other Bethlehem. This is a scene with which we are familiar in the grand old mosaics of the Roman Basilicas, a further development of Christian art, to which, as far as the choice of subjects is concerned and the mode of executing

Glass in the Vatican Library.
Representing Christ between SS. Peter and Paul; also Christ as the Lamb, and the faithful as Lambs—Jews and Gentiles coming from Jerusalem and Bethlehem (*Recle*) to Mount Sion, whence flow the four Evangelical Streams, united in the Mystical Jordan.

them, the sculpture may be considered a sort of intermediate step after the decline of painting.

We may still further add, that the cycle of scriptural subjects was somewhat enlarged by the sculptors;

at least, we do not know of any paintings in the Catacombs which represent our Lord giving sight to the blind, or raising the dead child to life, or healing the woman who touched the hem of His garment; or His nativity, His triumphant entry into Jerusalem, or certain scenes of His Passion; yet all these, and some others besides, may be seen carved on the old Christian monuments collected in the Lateran Museum at Rome and elsewhere. The sarcophagus which has the representation of the Nativity, and with the traditional ox and ass by the manger, has its own date upon it, A.D. 343; but, as we are not here writing a complete history of Christian art, it must suffice to have given this general idea of its earliest efforts both in painting and sculpture.

CHAPTER VI.

THEIR INSCRIPTIONS.

WHAT student of antiquity, or what merely intelligent observer of men and manners, is content to leave an old church or churchyard without first casting his eye over its monumental inscriptions? In like manner, we think our readers would justly complain if we bade them take leave of the Catacombs without saying a word about their epitaphs. And if the study of any considerable number of epitaphs anywhere is pretty sure to be rewarded by the discovery of something more or less interesting, how much more have we not a right to expect from the monuments of Roman Christianity during a period of three or four hundred years!

And truly, if all these monuments had been preserved and gathered together into one place, or, better still, had all been left in their original places, they would have formed an invaluable and inexhaustible library for the Christian archæologist. This, however, has not been their lot. Hundreds and thousands of them have been destroyed by those who have broken into the Catacombs from time to time during the last thousand years, and drawn from them materials for building. Others, again, and amongst them some of the most valuable, have been given to learned antiquarians or devout ecclesiastics, who coveted them for their own private possession, and carried them off to their own distant homes, without reflecting upon the grievous injury which they were thus inflicting upon those that should come after them. A much larger number have been most injudiciously placed, even by persons who knew their value, and were anxious for their preservation, in the pavements of Roman churches, where they have been either gradually effaced by the constant tread of worshippers, or thoughtlessly removed and lost sight of on occasion of some subsequent restoration of this portion of the church. A few have been more securely placed in the museums of the Capitol and of the Roman College, in the porticoes of some of the Roman churches, or in the cloisters of convents. Lastly, twelve or thirteen hundred were brought together, some eighty or ninety years ago, in the Library and Lapidarian Gallery at the Vatican—a number sufficiently great to enable us to appreciate their value, and to increase our regret that so many more should have been dispersed and lost.

It is to the sovereign Pontiffs that we are principally indebted for whatever fragments have been preserved from the general wreck. As early as the middle of the fifteenth century, Pope Nicholas V. seems to have entertained the idea of collecting all the lapidarian monuments of early Christianity which had at that time been discovered; and both Eugenius IV., his immediate predecessor, and Calixtus III. who succeeded him, forbade, under heavy penalties, the alienation or destruction of anything belonging to this class of monuments. When Leo X., too, appointed Raphael to superintend the works at the rebuilding of St. Peter's, he gave him a special charge that the *res lapidaria* should not be injured. In later times, these injunctions became more earnest and more frequent, in proportion to the increasing number and importance of the inscriptions that were brought to light. Still nothing practical appears to have been devised until the reign of Benedict XIV., who appointed the learned Francesco Bianchini to collect all the inscribed stones that could be found; and it was he who recommended the long narrow gallery leading to the Vatican Library and Museum as a convenient place for their preservation. Even then political and other difficulties interfered to prevent the execution of the design, so that it was not until the close of the last century that it was really carried out by Gaetano Marini, under the orders of Pope Pius VI. It is to be regretted that he took so little pains to make the most of such materials as he had. He merely inserted the monuments in the wall, without giving any indication of the places where they had been found, or making any attempts to classify them, beyond separating the few which contain the names of the consuls from those which are without this chronological note. A small selection has since been made, in our own day, by De Rossi, in obedience to the orders of Pope Pius IX., and placed in a gallery of the Lateran Palace, adjoining the Christian Museum. The arrangement of these specimens (few as they are, comparatively speaking) makes it a valuable guide to those who would study this part of our subject to any profit.

The collections at the Vatican and the Lateran together do not exceed two thousand. Hundreds of others, recovered by more recent excavations, have not yet found a suitable home; many have been left in their original sites. Still it will always remain true that the number actually in existence is quite insignificant when compared with those which have been destroyed or lost. A large proportion, however, even of these have not altogether perished; they were copied, not always with accuracy, yet with praiseworthy diligence, by various scholars, even from the eighth and ninth centuries; and since the invention of printing, similar collections have been, of course, more frequent. We need not enter into any detailed account of these; we will say but a brief word even about De Rossi's collection, for as yet he has only published the first volume, which contains all the Christian inscriptions of Rome during the first six centuries, whose date is indisputably fixed by the names of the consuls having been appended to them.

Of these, only one belongs to the first century, two to the second, the third supplies twenty, and the fourth and fifth about five hundred each. Of this last century, of course, only those which belong to the first ten years can be claimed for the Catacombs, because, as we have already seen, they ceased after that period to be the common cemetery of the faithful. It appears, then, that all the dated inscriptions of gravestones found in the Catacombs up to the year 1864 do not amount to six hundred: whence some writers have argued that in the earliest ages Christians were not in the habit of inscribing epitaphs on their graves. This conclusion, however, is obviously illogical; for we have no right to assume that the proportion between dated and undated inscriptions remained uniform during the first four centuries. If there are only six hundred epitaphs bearing the names of consuls, there are more than twice as many thousands without those names; and we must seek, by independent processes of inquiry, to establish other chronological criteria, which, if not equally exact, may yet be shown to be generally trustworthy. And this is what De Rossi has done, with a zeal tempered by caution which is beyond all praise. It would be impossible to exaggerate, first, the slow and patient industry with which he has accumulated observations; then the care and assiduity with which he compares the innumerable examples he has collected with one another, so as to ascertain their marks of resemblance and difference; and finally, the moderation with which he has drawn his conclusions. These vary in value, from mere conjecture to the highest degree of probability, or even of moral certainty. In a popular work like this, there is no room for discussion; we must confine ourselves to a statement of some of the best ascertained and most important facts, resting upon certain chronological canons, which a daily increasing experience warrants us in saying are now demonstrated with palpable and almost mathematical exactness.

First, then, De Rossi observes it as a notable fact, attested by the contents of all the Catacombs, that the most ancient inscriptions on Christian tombs differ from those of the Pagans " more by what they do *not* say, than by what they do say." The language of Christian epigraphy was not created in a day any more than Christian art was. There were urgent reasons for changing or omitting what the Pagans had been wont to use; but the Church did not at once provide anything else in its stead. Hence the very earliest Christian tombstones only recorded the bare name or names of the deceased, to which, in a *very few* instances, chiefly of ladies, one or two words, or the initials of words, were added, to denote the rank or title which belonged to them—*e.g.*, C.F., *clarissima femina*, or lady of senatorial rank. Generally speaking, however, there is an entire absence from these epitaphs of all those titles of rank and dignity with which Pagan monuments are so commonly overloaded. And the same must be said of those titles also which belong to the other extremity of the social scale, such as *servus* and *libertus*. One cannot study a dozen monuments of Pagan Rome without coming across some trace of this great social division of the ancient world into freemen and slaves. Yet in a number of Christian inscriptions in Rome, exceeding twelve or thirteen thousand, and all belonging to centuries during which slavery still flourished, scarcely ten have been found—and even two or three of these are doubtful — containing any allusion whatever to this fundamental division of ancient Roman society. It is not to be supposed that there was any legislation upon the subject; not even, perhaps, a hint from the clergy; it was simply the spontaneous effect of the religious doctrines of the new society, reflected in their epigraphy as in a faithful mirror. The children of the Primitive Church did not record on their monuments titles of earthly dignity, because they knew that with the God whom they served there was no respect of persons; neither did they care to mention the fact of their bondage, or of their deliverance from bondage, to some earthly master, because they thought only of that higher and more perfect liberty "wherewith Christ had set them free;" remembering that "he that was called, being a bondman, was yet a freeman of the Lord; and likewise he that was called, being free, was still the bondman of Christ."

We repeat, then, that the most ancient inscriptions on Christian gravestones in Rome consisted merely of the name of the deceased; ordinarily his *cognomen* only, though in some of the very earliest date the name of the *gens* was also added; not, we may be sure, from a motive of vanity, but merely for the purpose of identification. Large groups of inscriptions of this kind may still be seen in some of the oldest portions of subterranean Rome; traced in vermilion on the tiles, as in the Catacomb of Sta. Priscilla, or engraved in letters of most beautiful classical form, as in the Cœmeterium Ostrianum and the Cemetery of Pretextatus. The names are often of classical origin; nearly a hundred instances of Claudii, Flavii, Ulpii, Aurelii, and others of the same date, carrying us back to the period between Nero and the first of the Antonines. Very often there is added after the names, as on Pagan tombstones, such words as *filio dulcissimo, conjugi dulcissimo,* or, *incomparabili, dulcissimis parentibus,* and nothing else. In fact, these epitaphs vary so little from the old classical type, that had they not been seen by Marini and other competent witnesses — some of them even by De Rossi himself — in their original position, and some of them been marked with the Christian symbol of the anchor, we might have hesitated whether they ought not rather to be classed among Pagan monuments; as it is, we are sure that they belonged to the earliest Christian period; that they are the gravestones of men who died in the Apostolic, or immediately post-Apostolic age.

It was not to be expected, however, that Christian epitaphs should always remain so brief and bare a record. In the light of Christian doctrine, death had altogether changed its character; it was no longer an everlasting sleep, though here and there a Christian epitaph may still be found to call it so; it was no longer a final and perpetual separation from those who were left behind; it was recognised as the necessary gate of admission to a new and nobler life; and it was only likely, therefore, that some tokens of this change of feeling and belief should, sooner or later, find expression in the places where the dead were laid. Amid the almost innumerable monumental inscriptions of Pagan Rome that have been preserved to us, we seek in vain for any token of belief in a future life. Generally speaking, there is a total silence on the subject; but if the silence is broken, it is by faint traces of poetical imagery, not by the distinct utterances of a firm hope, much less of a clear and certain belief. The Christian epitaphs first broke this silence by the frequent use of a symbol, the anchor indicating hope, carved or rudely scratched beside the name upon the gravestone. Presently they added words also; words which were the natural outpourings of hearts which were full of Christian faith and love. On a few gravestones in those parts of the Catacomb of Sta. Priscilla already spoken of, we read the Apostolic salutation, *Pax tecum*, or *Pax tibi;* on one in the Cœmeterium Ostrianum, *Vivas in Deo,* and these are the first germs, out of which Christian epigraphy grew.

The epitaphs on the gravestones of the latter half of the second and of the third centuries are only a development of the fundamental ideas contained in these ejaculations. They still keep silence as to the worldly rank, or the Christian virtues of the deceased; they do not even, for the most part, tell us anything as to his age, or his relationship to the survivor who sets up the stone; most commonly, not even the day of his death or burial. But they announce with confident assurance that his soul has been admitted to that happy lot reserved for the just who have left this world in peace, that he is united with the saints, that he is in God, and in the enjoyment of good things; or they breathe a humble and loving prayer that he may soon be admitted to a participation in these blessings. They ask for the departed soul peace, and light, and refreshment, and rest in God and in Christ. Sometimes, also, they invoke the help of his prayers (since he, they know, still lives in God) for the surviving relatives whose time of trial is not yet ended. In a word, they proceed upon the assumption that there is an incessant interchange of kindly offices between this world and the next, between the living and the dead; they represent all the faithful as living members of one Body, the Body of Christ; as forming one great family, knit together in the closest bonds of love; and this love finding its chief work and happiness in prayer, prayer of the survivors for those who have gone before, prayer of the blessed for those who are left behind. We subjoin a few examples of the class of epitaphs of which we speak; and to secure accuracy, we will only give those that we have ourselves copied from the originals, and which every visitor to Rome may, therefore, still see if he pleases. The figures which we have appended to some of these inscriptions denote the column and the number under which they will be found in the gallery at the Lateran; the letters K.M. refer to the Kircherian Museum at the Roman College; and the last four may be seen where they were found, in the Catacomb of SS. Nereus and Achilles.

1. PAX TECUM, URANIA. xviii. 17.
2. SPES, PAX TIBI. xviii. 20.
3. ΥΓΙΕΙΑ ΖΗΣΕΣ ΜΕΤΑ ΙΣΤΕΡΚΟΡΙΟΥ
ΤΟΥ ΛΕΓΟΜΕΝΟΥ ΥΓΕΙΝΟΥ ΕΝ ΤΕΩ. xix. 23.
4. ΦΙΓΟΤΜΕΝΗ ΕΝ ΕΙΡΗΝΗ ΣΟΥ ΤΟ ΠΝΕΥΜΑ. ix. 28.
5. LAIS CUM PACE. ISPIRITUS IN BONU QUESCAT. ix. 15.
6. SUSANNA VIVAS IN DEO. xx. 30.
7. SEMPER IN D. VIVAS, DULCIS ANIMA. ix. 5.
8. REGINA, VIVAS IN DOMINO ZESU. ix. 17.
9. BOLOSA, DEUS TIBI REFRIGERET QUÆ VIXIT ANNOS XXXI. ix. 12.
10. AMERIMNUS RUFINÆ. . . . SPIRITUM TUUM DEUS REFRIGERET. ix. 13.
11. REFRIGERA DEUS ANIMA HO . . . ix. 14.
12. KALEMERE DEUS REFRIGERET SPIRITUM TUUM
UNA CUM SORORIS TUÆ HILARE. K. M.
13. LUCIFERE . . . MERUIT TITULUM
INSCRIBI UT QUISQUI DE FRATRIBUS LEGERIT ROGET DEU
UT SANCTO ET INNOCENTI SPIRITO AD DEUM SUSCIPIATUR. ix. 10.

14. ANATOLIUS FILIO BENEMERENTI FECIT
    QUI VIXIT ANNIS VII MENSIS VII DIEBUS XX
    ISPIRITUS TUUS BENE REQUIESCAT
    IN DEO. PETAS PRO SORORE TUA. viii. 19.
15. AURELIVS AGAPETVS ET AURELIA
    FELICISSIMA ALVMNE FELICITATI
    DIGNISSIMÆ QVE VICSIT ANIS XXX ET VI
    ET PETE PRO CELSINIANV COJVGEM. viii. 21.
16. PETE PRO PARENTES TVOS
    MATRONATA MATRONA
    QVE VIXIT AN. I. DI. LIII. viii. 18.
17. ΔΙΟΝΥCΙΟC ΝΗΠΙΟC ΑΚΑΚΟC ΕΝΘΑΔΕ
    ΚΕΙΤΕ ΜΕΤΑ ΤΩΝ ΑΓΙΩΝ ΜΝΗCΚΕCΘΕ
    ΔΕ ΚΑΙ ΗΜΩΝ ΕΝ ΤΑΙC ΑΓΙΑΙC ΥΜΩΝ
    ΠΡΕΥΧΑΙC ΚΑΙ ΤΟΥ ΓΑΤΨΑΤΟC ΚΑΙ
          ΓΡΑΨΑΝΤΟC. Κ. Μ.
18. GENTIANVS FIDELIS IN PACE QVI VIX
    IT ANNIS XXI MENNS VIII DIES
    XVI ET IN ORATIONIS TVIS
    ROGES PRO NOBIS QVIA SCIMVS TE IN ☧. (Vatican Gallery.)
19. ΔΗΜΗΤΡΙC ΕΤ ΛΕΟΝΤΙΑ
    CΕΙΡΙΚΕ ΦΕΙΛΙΕ ΒΕΝΕΜΕΡΕΝ
    ΤΙ ΜΝΗCΘΗC ΙΗCΟΥC
    Ο ΚΥΡΙΟC ΤΕΚΝΟΝ Ε . . .
20. VICTORIA REFRIGER
    ISSPIRITUS TUS IN BONO.
21. . . . VIBAS IN PACE ET PETE PRO NOBIS,
22. ΖΗCΑΙC ΕΝ K͞Ω ΚΑΙ ΕΡΩΤΑ ΥΠΕΡ ΗΜΩΝ.

1. Peace with thee, Urania.
2. Peace to thee, Spes.
3. Hygeia, mayest thou live in God with Stercorius, who is (also) called Hyginus.
4. Beloved one, may thy spirit be in peace.
5. Peace with thee, Lais. May thy spirit rest in good [*i.e.*, God].
6. Susanna, mayest thou live in God.
7. Sweet soul, mayest thou always live in God.
8. Regina, mayest thou live in the Lord Jesus.
9. Bolosa, may God refresh thee; who lived thirty-one years.
10. Amerimnus . . . to Rufina, may the Lord refresh thy spirit.
11. Refresh, O God, the soul of . . .
12. Kalemere, may God refresh thy spirit, together with that of thy sister Hilare.

13. Lucifera ... deserved that an epitaph should be inscribed to her, that whoever of the brethren shall read it, may pray God that her holy and innocent spirit may be received to God.
14. Anatolius set this up to his well-deserving son, who lived seven years, seven months, and twenty days. May thy spirit rest well in God. Pray for thy sister.
15. Aurelius Agapetus and Aurelia Felicissima to their most excellent foster-child Felicitas, who lived thirty-six years; and pray for your husband Celsinianus.
16. Pray for your parents, Matronata Matrona, who lived one year and fifty-three days.
17. Dionysius, an innocent child, lies here with the saints: and remember us, too, in your holy prayers, both me who engraved and me who wrote [this inscription].
18. Gentianus, one of the faithful, in peace, who lived twenty-one years, eight months, and sixteen days: and in your prayers make petition for us, because we know that thou art in Christ.
19. Demetrius and Leontia to their well-deserving daughter Syrica. Remember, O Lord Jesus, our child.
20. Victoria, may thy spirit be refreshed in good [*i.e.*, in God].
21. Mayest thou live in peace and pray for us.
22. Mayest thou live in the Lord and pray for us.

It would be easy to fill several pages with inscriptions of this kind; but enough has been produced to impress upon the reader a fair idea of their general character. They abound on the monuments of the second and third centuries; but after that date they fade out of use, and are succeeded by a new style of epigraphy, colder and more historical. Mention is now made of the exact age of the deceased, and of the length of his married life, not as to years only, but as to months, and sometimes even as to days and hours; of the day of his death also, more commonly of his burial, and, in a few instances, of both. To record the day of the burial (*depositio*) was creeping into use before the end of the third century; from the middle of the fourth, it became little short of universal; and in this century and the next, mention of the year also was frequently added. During this period, the phrase *in pace* became general, as a formula to be used by itself absolutely without any verb at all. In old Christian inscriptions in Africa, this phrase frequently occurs with the verb *vixit*; in which case the word *pax* is undoubtedly used in the same sense in which Tertullian, St. Cyprian, and other ecclesiastical writers employ it, as denoting peace with God to be obtained through communion with the Church; and in a community distracted by schisms and heresies, as the African Church was, such a record on the tomb of a Christian is intelligible and important. Not so in Rome; here the purport of the thousands of greetings of peace has reference to the peace of a joyful resurrection and a happy eternity, whether spoken of with confidence as already possessed, or only prayed for with glad expectation. The act of death had been expressed in earlier epitaphs under Christian phrases:—*Translatus de sæculo; exivit de sæculo; arcessitus a Domino*, or *ab angelis; natus in æternum;* or, much more commonly, *Deo reddidit spiritum;* and this last phrase had come into such established use by the middle of the third century, that the single letter R was a recognised abbreviation of it. But, in the second half of that century, and still more frequently afterwards *decessit* was used in its stead; and in the fifth century we find this again superseded by *Hic jacet, pausat, quiescit*, or *requiescit*.

Complimentary phrases as to the goodness, wisdom, innocence, and holiness of the deceased came into fashion about the age of Constantine, and in later times were repeated with such uniformity as to be quite wearisome; we see that they were simply formal and unmeaning; not unfrequently they were extravagant. Widows and widowers bear mutual testimony to one another's gentleness and amiability of disposition, which enabled them to live together so many years *semper concordes, sine ullâ querelâ, sine læsione animi*. But this was, after all, only a return to the style of Pagan epigraphy, in which the very same phrases were frequently used. Children are commended for innocence and simplicity of spirit; sometimes also for wisdom and beauty! A child of five years old is *miræ bonitatis et totius innocentiæ*. This belongs to the year 387. In the next century, we find, for the first time, the phrase *contra votum*, which was also a return to the language of Pagan parents when burying their children. It cannot be said that there is anything absolutely unchristian in this phrase; at the same time, it does not savour of that hearty resignation to the will of God, or that cheerful assertion of His providence, to be found in other epitaphs; as, for instance, in more than a score of inscriptions recovered from the ancient cemetery in Ostia, in which this resignation is touchingly expressed by the statement that the deceased had ended his term of days "*when God willed it.*"

Of course, there still remains very much more that might be said, and which it would be interesting to say, about the thousands of inscriptions that have been found in the Catacombs; but we can only here attempt to indicate the main outlines of the subject, and enough has been said to satisfy our readers that Christian epigraphy followed the same laws of development as Christian art. At first it resembled the corresponding monuments of Paganism, excepting in those particulars in which Christian dogma and Christian feeling suggested a departure from that model. Still for a while that dogma and feeling found no distinct positive expression. Then it began to whisper, at first in hidden symbols, such as the dove, the anchor, and the fish; then, in the short but hearty apostolic salutation, *Pax tecum*, *Pax tibi*, *Vivas in Deo*, and the like. By and by these pious ejaculations, dictated by a spirit of affectionate piety towards the deceased, and a tender solicitude for his eternal welfare, became more frequent and less laconic; and so, step by step, a special style of Christian epigraphy grows up spontaneously (as it were) out of the joyful light of faith and hope of heaven. A certain type becomes fixed, varying indeed, as all things human never fail to vary, in some minor details, according to circumstances of time and place, or the peculiar tastes and fancies of this or that individual, yet sufficiently consistent to set a distinctive mark upon each particular period, whilst by its variations during successive ages it faithfully reflects (we may be sure) some corresponding change in the tone and temper of the ordinary Christian mind. Christian epigraphy was born as Christian art was, simultaneously with the introduction of Christianity itself into the metropolis of the ancient world; it acquired all its special characteristics, and perhaps attained its highest religious perfection, before the end of the third century, after which its beautiful and touching simplicity is somewhat marred and secularised by a gradual influx of some of those modes of thought and expression which prevailed in the world without.

Part Second.

CHAPTER I.

THE PAPAL CRYPT.

WE have now acquired a sufficient general idea of the Catacombs to enable us to understand what we see when we come to examine any one of them in detail; and we will, therefore, proceed to pay a visit to the famous Cemetery of Callixtus.

But first we must explain what is meant by this title. It may be used in two senses. When first the Catacombs were made, and as long as the true history of their origin and gradual development was remembered, "the Cemetery of Callixtus" was only a small and well-defined area, measuring 250 Roman feet by 100, and situated on a little cross-road which united the Via Appia with the Via Ardeatina. But as time went on, other areæ were joined to this, until at length a vast and intricate subterranean necropolis was formed, measuring several hundred feet both in length and breadth; and to the whole of this space, for convenience' sake, we continue to give the name of one of its most ancient and famous parts. In our visit we shall pass through some portions of several of these areæ; for we shall first descend into the original "Cemetery of Callixtus," and we shall return to the upper world from the "Crypt of Lucina," which in the old martyrologies is spoken of as "near" that cemetery, not as part of it.

The casual visitor cannot, of course, expect to be able to distinguish the limits of the several areæ which he traverses in his hurried subterranean walk;

Galleries in Cemetery of St. Callixtus breaking through graves.

nevertheless, if he keeps his eyes open, he cannot fail to recognise occasional tokens of the transition; as, for instance, when he finds himself passing from a higher to a lower level, or *vice versâ*, or when the path which he is pursuing leads him through a wall of broken graves, so that it has been necessary perhaps to strengthen the points of connection by masonry. Any one who desires to study this branch of the subject, will find it fully treated of, and made easily intelligible, by numerous plans and illustrations either in the original work of De Rossi, or in the English abridgment of it. The present popular manual proposes to itself a more humble task. We propose to describe the principal objects of interest which are shown to strangers, and to supply such historical or archæological information as will give them a greater interest in, and a keener appreciation of, the importance of what they see.

Without further preface, then, let us set out on our walk. Let us proceed along the Via Appia till we come to a doorway on the right-hand side, over which we read the words "Cœmeterium S. Callixti." On entering the vineyard our attention is first arrested by a ruined monument standing close beside us. We shall have already seen others more or less like it on both sides of the road since we came out of the city; and in answer to our inquiries we shall have learnt that they are the remains of what were once grand Pagan tombs, covered, probably, with marble and ornamented with sculpture. Without stopping then to inquire whether anything special is known about the history of this particular mausoleum, we will walk forward to another more modest building standing in the middle of the vineyard. It looks small and mean; and if we could enter it, we should find that it is used only as a convenient magazine for the stowing away of fragments of sarcophagi, or tombstones, extracted from the cemetery which underlies it. Yet its apsidal termination, and the other apses on either side of the building, naturally suggest to us that it must once have had something of an ecclesiastical character. In truth, it was one of the "numerous buildings constructed throughout the cemeteries" by Fabian, pope and martyr, in the middle of the third century (see page 27), and was

Entrance to the Cemetery of St. Callixtus.

known to ancient pilgrims as the *cella memoriæ*, or chapel of St. Sixtus and of St. Cæcilia, being built immediately over the tombs of those martyrs. Originally, the end or fourth side of the building was unenclosed, that so larger numbers of the faithful might assist at the celebration of the holy mysteries: indeed the side-walls themselves were not at first continued to their present length, but the building consisted of little else than the three *exedræ* or apses.

If we examine the ground round this ancient chapel, we shall see that it was once used as a place of burial. All round it, but not within it, nor yet quite close to its walls, but just at a sufficient distance from them to allow space for the channels which carried off the water from the roof (traces of which channels still remain), deep graves are dug, of various sizes, but all arranged according to a regular plan of orientation. These graves are made chiefly with blocks of tufa; but bricks also are used, and thick layers of mortar. Some of them were cased inside with marble, or at least had slabs of that material at the top and bottom, the upper surface of the one serving as the bottom of another; and it is worthy of remark that on several of these slabs were inscribed epitaphs of the usual kind, though their position would necessarily conceal them from every human eye. Some of the graves were made of sufficient depth to receive ten bodies, one over the other; some could only receive four; and occasionally only a single sarcophagus occupied the grave. The average, however, may be taken at four bodies in each grave, which would give a total of eight thousand persons buried over the first area of the Catacomb of St. Callixtus. Of course this cemetery, being in the open air, is no part of the catacomb —properly so called; it is of later date, having been made in the fourth and fifth centuries, but it observes precisely the same limits as the catacomb. The boundary-wall may still be seen at no great distance from the chapel; and beyond it no graves are to be found either in the cemetery or in the catacomb; a fact which shows with what care the rights of private property were respected below ground as well as above.

But now let us no longer tarry in the open air, but go down at once into the catacomb. A staircase stands ready at our side, being in fact a mere restoration of the original entrance. When we get to the bottom, a keen eye may detect upon the plaster of the walls a certain number of *graffiti*, as they are called, or scribblings of names, ejaculations, &c., of very great antiquity. It is comparatively a new thing to pay any attention to these rude scribblings of ancient visitors on the walls of places of public resort, and to take pains to decipher them; but of late years they have proved to be a most interesting subject of study, whether found on the tombs of Egyptian kings in Thebes, on the walls of the barracks and theatres in Pompeii, in the prisons and cellars of Pagan Rome, or, lastly, in the Christian Catacombs. Here especially they have proved to be of immense importance, being, as De Rossi justly calls them, "the faithful echo of history and infallible guides through the labyrinth of subterranean galleries;" for by means of them we can trace the path that was followed by pilgrims to subterranean Rome from the fourth to the seventh century, and identify the crypts or chapels which were most frequently visited. Probably there is no group of ancient *graffiti* in the world to be compared, either for number or intricacy, with those which cover the wall at the entrance of the crypt we are about to enter; and it must have been a work of infinite labour to disentangle and decipher them. Now that the work has been done for us, however, by the indefatigable De Rossi, we can see that they may be divided into three classes. They are either the mere names of persons, with the occasional adjunct of their titles; or they are good wishes, prayers, salutations, or acclamations, on behalf of friends and relatives, living or dead; or, lastly, they are invocations of the martyrs near whose tombs they are inscribed.

Of the names we find two kinds; one, the most ancient and most numerous, scribbled on the first coat of plaster, and in the most convenient and accessible parts of the wall, are names of the old classical type, such as Tychis, Elpidephorus, Polyneicus, Maximus, Nikasius, and the like; the other, belonging manifestly to a somewhat later period, because written on a later coat of plaster, and in more inaccessible places, high above the first, are such as Lupo, Ildebrand, Ethelrid, Bonizo, Joannes Presb., Prando Pr., *indignus peccator*, &c., &c.

Prayers or acclamations for absent or departed friends are mixed among the most ancient names, and generally run in the same form as the earliest and most simple Christian epitaphs, *e.g.*, VIVAS, VIVAS IN DEO CRISTO, VIVAS IN ETERNO, ZHC EN

ΘΕΩ, BIBAC IN ΘΕΩ, TE IN PACE, &c. "Mayest thou live in God Christ, for ever, Thee in peace," &c. The feeling which prompted the pilgrims who visited these shrines thus to inscribe in sacred places the names of those they loved and would fain benefit, is so natural to the human heart, that instances of it may be found even among the heathen themselves.

But besides mere names and short acclamations, there are also in the same place, and manifestly belonging to a very early age, prayers and invocations of the martyrs who lay buried in these chapels. Sometimes the holy souls of all the martyrs are addressed collectively, and petitioned to hold such or such an one in remembrance; and sometimes this prayer is addressed to one individually. The following may suffice as specimens:—MARCIANUM SUCCESSUM SEVERUM SPIRITA SANCTA IN MENTE HAVETE, ET OMNES FRATRES NOSTROS. PETITE SPIRITA SANCTA UT VERECUNDUS CUM SUIS BENE NAVIGET. OTIA PETITE ET PRO PARENTE ET PRO FRATRIBUS EJUS; VIBANT CUM BONO. SANTE SUSTE, IN MENTE HABEAS IN HORATIONES AURELIU REPENTINU. ΔΙΟΝΤΣΙΝ ΕΙΣ ΜΝΙΑΝ ΕΧΕΤΑΙ (for EXETE). "Holy souls, have in remembrance Marcianus Successus Severus and all our brethren. Holy souls, ask that Verecundus and his friends may have a prosperous voyage. Ask for rest both for my parent and his brethren; may they live with good Holy Sixtus, have in remembrance in your prayers

Aurelius Repentinus. Have ye in remembrance Dionysius."

The inspection of these *graffiti*, then, is enough to warn us that we are on the threshold of a very special sanctuary of the ancient Church, and to excite our deepest interest in all that we may find it to contain. But our first impression on entering will probably be one of disappointment. We were led to expect that we were about to visit a Christian burial-place and place of worship of very great antiquity, but the greater part of the masonry we see around us is manifestly of quite recent construction. The truth is, that when this chamber was rediscovered in 1854, it was in a complete state of ruin; access was gained to it only through the *luminare*, which, as usual, had served for many centuries as a channel for pouring into it all the adjacent soil, fragments of grave-stones from the cemetery above-ground, decaying brick-work, and every kind of rubbish. When this was removed, the vault of the chamber, deprived of its usual support, soon gave way; so that, if any portion of it was to be preserved and put in a condition to be visited with safety, it was absolutely necessary to build fresh walls, and otherwise strengthen it. This has been done with the utmost care, and so as still to preserve, wherever it was possible, remains of the more ancient condition of the chapel and of its decoration in succeeding ages. Thus we are able to trace very clearly in the arch of the doorway three stages or conditions of ornamentation by means of three different coatings of plaster, each retaining some remnant of its original painting. We can trace also the remains of the marble slabs with which, at a later period, the whole chapel was faced; and even this *later* period takes us back to the earlier half of the fifth century, when, as the *Liber Pontificalis* tells us, St. Sixtus III. *platoniam fecit in Cœmeterio Callixti*. The fragments of marble columns and other ornamental work, which lie scattered about on the pavement, belong probably to the same period, or they may have been the work of St. Leo III., the last pontiff of whom we read that he made restorations here before the translation of the relics by Pope Paschal I. Again, the raised step or dais of marble, which we see directly opposite to us at the further end of the chapel, having four holes or sockets in it, was of course found here as it now is, and it shows plainly where the altar once stood, supported on four pillars; but in the wall behind this platform we seem to detect traces of a yet older and more simple kind of altar—a sepulchre hewn out of the rock, the flat covering of which was probably the original *mensa* whereon the holy mysteries were celebrated in this place.

Thus, spite of the ruin and the neglect of ages, and spite of the work of restoration which has been thereby made necessary in our own time, many clear traces still remain both of its original condition and of the reverent care with which successive generations of the ancient Church did their best to adorn this chamber. The cause of this extraordinary and long-continued veneration is revealed to us, in part, by a few grave-stones which have been recovered from amid the rubbish, and which are now restored, if not to the precise spots they originally occupied (which we cannot tell), yet certainly to the *walls* in which they were first placed; in part also by an inscription of Pope Damasus, which, though broken into more than a hundred pieces, has yet been put together from the fragments discovered in this chamber, the few words or letters that have not been found being supplied in letters of a different colour; the whole, therefore, may now again be read just where our forefathers in the faith read it when it was first set up 1500 years ago. The tombstones are of St. Anteros and St. Fabian, who sat in the chair of Peter from A.D. 235 to 250; of St. Lucius, A.D. 252; and of St. Eutychianus, who died nearly thirty years later. No one having an intimate acquaintance with Christian epigraphy doubts that these are the original grave-stones of the Popes whose names they bear; and it is certain that other Popes of the same century were buried here also; but as their tombstones are not before our eyes, we will say nothing about them in this place, but go on to speak of the inscription of Pope Damasus. It runs in this wise:—

HIC CONGESTA JACET QUÆRIS SI TURBA PIORUM,
CORPORA SANCTORUM RETINENT VENERANDA SEPULCHRA,
SUBLIMES ANIMAS RAPUIT SIBI REGIA CŒLI:

HIC COMITES XYSTI PORTANT QUI EX HOSTE TROPÆA;
HIC NUMERUS PROCERUM SERVAT QUI ALTARIA CHRISTI;
HIC POSITUS LONGA VIXIT QUI IN PACE SACERDOS;
HIC CONFESSORES SANCTI QUOS GRÆCIA MISIT;
HIC JUVENES, PUERIQUE, SENES CASTIQUE NEPOTES,
QUÏS MAGE VIRGINEUM PLACUIT RETINERE PUDOREM.
HIC FATEOR DAMASUS VOLUI MEA CONDERE MEMBRA,
SED CINERES TIMUI SANCTOS VEXARE PIORUM.

"Here, if you would know, lie heaped together a whole crowd of saints.
These honoured sepulchres enclose their bodies,
Their noble souls the palace of Heaven has taken to itself.
Here lie the companions of Xystus, who triumphed over the enemy;
Here a number of rulers, who keep the altars of Christ;
Here is buried the Bishop, who lived in a long peace;
Here the holy Confessors whom Greece sent us;
Here lie youths and boys, old men, and their chaste relatives,
Who chose, as the better part, to keep their virgin chastity.
Here I, Damasus, confess I wished to lay my bones,
But I feared to disturb the holy ashes of the saints."

The first lines of this inscription seem to allude to a number of martyrs laid together in one large tomb, such as we know from other witnesses were sometimes to be seen in the Roman Catacombs. The poet Prudentius, for instance, supposes a friend to ask him the names of those who have shed their blood for the faith in Rome, and the epitaphs inscribed on their tombs. He replies that it would be very difficult to tell this, for that "the relics of the saints in Rome are innumerable, since as long as the city continued to worship their Pagan gods, their wicked rage slew vast multitudes of the just. On many tombs, indeed," he says, "you may read the name of the martyr, and some short inscription; but there are many others which are silent as to the name, and only express the number. You can ascertain the number which lie heaped up together (*congestis corpora acervis*), but nothing more;" and he specifies one grave in particular, in which he learnt that the relics of sixty martyrs had been laid, but their names were known only to Christ. To some such *polyandrium*, then, the words of Pope Damasus would seem to allude, and the martyrologies and other ancient documents speak of three or four such tombs "near St. Cecilia's;" and here in this very chamber, just where (as we shall presently see) it touches the crypt of St. Cecilia, we can still recognise a pit of unusual size and depth, intended apparently for the reception of many bodies, or perhaps only of the charred remains of many bodies; for, where the victims were numerous, the capital sentence was not unfrequently executed by fire.

Of the martyrdom of St. Sixtus we have already spoken as having taken place in the Catacomb of Pretextatus (page 31), but his body was brought here to be laid with those of his predecessors. Pope Damasus only mentions his deacons, and not St. Sixtus himself, because he had composed another set of verses in honour of the holy Pontiff alone, and had set them up in this same crypt. It is easy to see where they were placed, above and behind the altar, and a copy of them has been preserved to us by ancient pilgrims and scholars. Scarcely a dozen letters of them, however, were found when the chapel was cleared out in 1854; they have not, therefore, been restored to their place, and need not be reproduced in this manual.

The *numerus procerum* in the fifth line of our present inscription are, of course, the Popes whose epitaphs we have seen, and others who were buried here; nor can we fail to recognise in the Bishop who enjoyed a long life of peace Pope Melchiades, who lived when the persecutions had ended. Finally, we have heard the story of some at least of "the holy confessors who came from Greece," Hippolytus Maria and Neo, Adrias and Paulina (page 37); and the *arenarium* in which these martyrs were buried was in the immediate neighbourhood of the Papal crypt which we are describing.

CHAPTER II.

THE CRYPT OF ST. CECILIA.

A NARROW doorway, cut somewhat irregularly through the rock in the corner of the Papal Crypt, introduces us into another chamber. As we pass through this doorway we observe that the sides were once covered with slabs of marble, and the arch over our heads adorned with mosaics. The chamber itself is much larger than that which we have left behind us. It is nearly 20 feet square (the other had been only 14 by 11); it is irregular in shape; it has a wide *luminare* over it, completely flooding it with light, and at the other end of it is a large portico, supported by arches of brick. Yet we see no altar-tomb, no contemporary epitaphs of popes or martyrs, nor indeed anything else which at once engages our attention and promises to give us valuable information. Nevertheless, a more careful examination will soon detect paintings and scribblings on the walls not inferior in interest to any that are to be seen elsewhere. We shall hardly appreciate them, however, as they deserve, unless we first briefly call to mind the history of the relics of St. Cecilia, before whose tomb we are.

We shall take it for granted that our readers are familiar with the history of the Saint's martyrdom, and pass on to the first discovery of her relics in the ninth century. Pope Paschal I. succeeded to the see of Peter in January A.D. 817, and in the following July he translated into different churches within the city the relics of 2300 martyrs, collected from the various suburban cemeteries, which, as we have seen, were lying at that time in a deplorable state of ruin. Amongst the relics thus removed were those of the popes from the Papal Crypt we have just visited. His cotemporary biographer, writing in the *Liber Pontificalis*, tells us that Paschal had wished to remove at the same time the body of St. Cecilia, which the Acts of her martyrdom assured him had been buried by Pope Urban "near to his own colleagues;" but he could not find it; so at length he reluctantly acquiesced in the report that it had been carried off by Astulfus, the Lombard king, by whom Rome had been besieged, and the cemeteries plundered. Some four years afterwards, however, St. Cecilia appeared to him in a dream or vision, as he was assisting at matins in the Vatican Basilica, and told him that when he was translating the bodies of the popes she was so close to him that they might have conversed together. In consequence of this vision he returned to the search, and found the body where he had been told. It was fresh and perfect as when it was first laid in the tomb, and clad in rich garments wrought with gold, lying in a cypress coffin, with linen cloths stained with blood rolled up at her feet.

It is not essential to our history, yet it may be worth while to add that Paschal tells us he lined the coffin with fringed silk, spread over the body a covering of silk gauze, and then, placing it within a sarcophagus of white marble, deposited it under the high altar of the Church of Sta. Cecilia in Trastevere, where it was rediscovered nearly eight hundred years afterwards (A.D. 1599) by the titular cardinal of the Church, and exposed to the veneration of the faithful

Maderna's Statue of St. Cecilia.

for a period of four or five weeks. All visitors to Rome have seen and admired Maderna's beautiful statue of the saint; but not all take sufficient notice of the legend which he has inserted around it, testifying that he was one of those who had seen her lying incorrupt in her coffin, and that he has reproduced her in marble, in the very same posture in which he saw her.

We have said that the Acts of the Saint's martyrdom assert that Pope Urban had buried her near to his own colleagues. The itineraries of ancient pilgrims mention her grave, either immediately before, or immediately after, those of the Popes. Finally, Pope Paschal says that he found her body close to the place whence he had withdrawn the bodies of his predecessors. Are these topographical notices true or false? This is the question which must have agitated the mind of De Rossi when he discovered this chamber so immediately contiguous to that in which he had learnt for certain that the Popes had been buried; or rather—for his own conviction upon this subject had been already formed—would there be anything in the chamber itself to confirm his conclusion, and to establish it to the satisfaction of others? We may imagine with what eagerness he desired to penetrate it. But this could not be done at once. The chapel was full of earth, even to the very top of the *luminare*, and all this soil must first be removed, through the *luminare* itself. As the work of excavation proceeded, there came to light first, on the wall of the *luminare*, the figure of a woman in the usual attitude of prayer, but so indistinct as to baffle all attempts at identification. Below this there appeared a Latin cross between two sheep, which may still be seen, though these also are much faded. Still lower down the wall—the wall, that is, of the *luminare*, not of the chamber itself—we come upon the figures of three saints, executed apparently in the fourth, or perhaps even the fifth century; but they are all of men ; and as their names inscribed at the side show no trace of any connection with the history of St. Cecilia, we will postpone what we have to say about them for the present, and proceed with our work of clearance of the whole chamber.

As we come nearer to the floor, we find upon the wall, close to the entrance from the burial-place of the popes, a painting which may be attributed, perhaps, to the seventh century, of a woman, richly attired, with pearls hanging from her ears and entwined in her hair, necklaces and bracelets of pearls and gold; a white dress covered with a pink tunic ornamented with gold and silver flowers, and large roses springing out of the ground by her feet. Everything about the painting is rich, and bright, and gay, such as an artist of the seventh century might picture to himself that a Roman bride, of wealth and noble family, like St. Cecilia, ought to have been. Below this figure we come to a niche, such as is found in other parts of the Catacombs, to receive the large shallow vessels of oil, or precious unguents, which, in ancient times, were used to feed the lamps burning before the tombs of the martyrs. At the back of this niche is a large head of our Lord, represented according to the Byzantine type, and with rays of glory behind it in the form of a Greek cross. Side by side with this, but on the flat surface of the wall, is a figure of a bishop, in full pontifical dress, with his name inscribed, S. VRBANVS.

Examination of these paintings shows that they

were not the original ornaments of the place. The painting of St. Cecilia was executed on the surface of ruined mosaic work, portions of which may still be easily detected towards the bottom of the picture. The niche, too, in which our Lord's head is painted bears evident traces of having once been encased

Crypt of St. Cecilia.

with porphyry, and both it and the figure of St. Urban are so rudely done, that they might have been executed as late as the tenth or eleventh century. Probably they belong to the age of the translation of the relics—*i.e.*, the ninth century. A half-obliterated scroll or tablet by the side of the figure of St. Urban states that it was intended as an ornament to the martyr's sepulchre—DECORI SEPULCRI S. CÆCILIÆ MARTYRIS. When we add that immediately by the side of these paintings is a deep recess in the wall, capable of receiving a large sarcophagus, and that between the back of this recess and the back of one of the papal graves in the adjoining chamber, there is scarcely an inch of rock, we think the most sceptical of critics will confess that the old traditions are very remarkably confirmed.

It will be asked, however, if this is really the place where St. Cecilia was buried, and if Paschal really visited the adjoining chapel, how is it possible that he could have had any difficulty in finding her tomb? To this we reply, first, by reminding our readers of the condition in which the Catacombs were at that time: these translations of relics were being made, because the cemeteries in which they lay were utterly ruined. But, secondly, it is very possible that the doorway, or the recess, or both, may have been walled up or otherwise concealed, for the express purpose of baffling the search of the sacrilegious Lombards. Nor is this mere conjecture. Among the *débris* of this spot De Rossi has found several fragments of a wall, too thin ever to have been used as a means of support, but manifestly serviceable as a curtain of concealment; and, although, with that perfect candour and truthfulness which so enhances all his other merits, he adds that these fragments bear tokens of belonging to a later date, this does not prove that there had not been another wall of the same kind at

K

an earlier period; for he is able to quote from his own discoveries the instance of an *arcosolium* in another Catacomb, which was thus carefully concealed in very ancient times by the erection of a wall. However, be the true explanation of this difficulty what it may, our ignorance on this subject cannot be allowed to outweigh the explicit testimony of Paschal and the other ancient witnesses now so abundantly confirmed by modern discoveries.

But it may be objected yet once more, that there is an inscription in the Catacomb under the Basilica of St. Sebastian, more than a quarter of a mile off, which states that St. Cecilia was buried there. Most true, but consider the date of the inscription. It was set up by William de Bois-Ratier, Archbishop of Bourges, in the year 1609; and there are other inscriptions hard by, of the same or of a later date, which claim for the same locality the tombs of several popes, as well as of thousands of martyrs. The inscriptions were set up precisely during that age in which the Catacombs were buried in the most profound darkness and oblivion. We have already explained (page 50) how it came to pass that whilst the other ancient cemeteries were inaccessible and unknown, this one under the Church of St. Sebastian still remained partially open; and we can heartily sympathise with the religious feelings which prompted the good Archbishop and others to make an appeal to the devotion of the faithful not to lose the memory of those glorious martyrs who had certainly been buried in a Catacomb on this road, and at no great distance, yet not in this particular spot. But whilst we admire their piety, we cannot bow to their authority upon a topographical question, which they had no means of deciding, and in respect to which recent discoveries, as well as the testimony of more ancient documents, prove to a demonstration that they were certainly wrong.

Dismissing, then, all these objections, which it was quite right and reasonable to raise, but which, on critical examination, entirely disappear, we may rest assured that we have here certainly recovered the original resting-place of one of the most ancient and famous of Rome's virgin saints. Let us take one more look round the crypt before we leave it. If we examine the picture of the saint more closely, we shall find it defaced by a number of *graffiti*, which may be divided into two classes; the one class quite irregular, both as to place and style of writing, consisting only of the names of pilgrims who had visited the shrine, several of whom were not Romans but foreigners. Thus, one is named Hildebrandus, another Lupo, another is a Bishop Ethelred, and two write themselves down Spaniards. But the other class of *graffiti* is quite regular, arranged in four lines, and contains almost exclusively the names of priests; the only exceptions being that one woman appears amongst them, but it is added that she is the mother of the priest (Leo) who signs before her, and that the last signature of all is that of a *scriniarius*, or secretary. There is something about this arrangement of names which suggests the idea of an official act; neither can it be attributed to chance that several of the same names (including the unusual name of Mercurius, and written too in the same peculiar style, a mixture of square and of cursive letters) appear on the painting of St. Cornelius, presently to be visited in a catacomb under this same vineyard, whence his body was translated some thirty or forty years before St. Cecilia's. In both cases these priests probably signed as witnesses of the translation.

It only remains that we should fulfil our promise to say a word or two about those saints whose names and figures we saw in the *luminare*. They are three in number, St. Sebastian, St. Cyrinus, and St. Polycamus. We know of no other Sebastian that can be meant here but the famous martyr, whose basilica we have mentioned before as being not far off. Cyrinus, or Quirinus, was Bishop of Siscia in Illyria, and martyr. In the days of Prudentius his body lay in his own city, but when Illyria was invaded by the barbarians it was brought to Rome and buried in the Basilica of St. Sebastian about the year 420. Of Polycamus the history is altogether lost; neither ecclesiastical historians nor martyrologists have left us any record of his life. We know, however, from the Itineraries of the old pilgrims that there was the tomb of one Polycamus, a martyr, near that of St. Cecilia, and the same name appears among the martyrs whose relics were removed from the Catacombs to the churches within the city. It would seem then that the figures of these three saints were painted in the *luminare* of this chamber, only because they were saints to whom there was much devotion, and whose relics were lying at no great distance.

CHAPTER III.

THE CRYPT OF ST. EUSEBIUS.

FROM the crypt of St. Cecilia we pass through a modern opening in one of its walls to a short gallery which leads to the sacramental chapels—*i.e.*, to those chambers whose walls are decorated with a remarkable series of paintings having reference to the Sacraments of Baptism and the Holy Eucharist. These paintings, however, having been sufficiently described and commented upon in another place, we may take our leave of this first area of the Cemetery of Callixtus, and, ascending a short staircase, pass on through the broken wall of a chamber into a wide and lofty gallery, which brings us presently to the chief object of interest in the second area—viz., the crypt of St. Eusebius, Pope, A.D. 310. Just before we reach it, we shall see on our left hand the staircase by which it was anciently arrived at; and if we stop here for a moment and look around us, we shall recognise an example of what has been already mentioned, the exemplary care and prudence with which the pilgrims of old were guided in their subterranean visits. Walls were built, blocking up all paths but the right one, so that they should not go astray or lose themselves in the labyrinth which surrounded them. They must needs go forward till they arrived at two chapels, which stood opposite to one another on different sides of the gallery.

One of these chambers was about 9 feet by 12, the other considerably larger, 16 by 13. The one had evidently been the chief object of devotion; the other was added for the convenience of the worshippers. The smaller one had an arcosolium on each side as well as at the end, the one opposite the door being the most important of the three; and all of these tombs were once ornamented with mosaics and paintings, and the walls of the chamber with marble. All is now sadly ruined; but it is still possible to distinguish among the remains of the mosaic work over the principal arcosolium traces of a very common Christian symbol, a double-handed vessel, with a bird on either side of it; also certain winged figures, which probably represent the seasons, and a few other accessories of ornament; but the main figures and general design have perished. The walls of the opposite chamber were never cased with marble, so that the pilgrims were able to leave here the same tokens of their visits as they left at St. Sixtus'. The *graffiti* are of the same general character, but of a somewhat later date; the old forms of prayer have disappeared; most of the names and inscriptions are in Latin; and among the few that are Greek, there are symptoms of Byzantine peculiarities.

The chief object of interest, however, now remaining in these chambers is the epitaph which stands in the middle of the smaller room. Of course, this was not its original position; but it has been so placed, in order that we may see both sides of the stone without difficulty, for both are inscribed. The stone was originally used for an inscription in honour of Caracalla, belonging to the year 214. The Christian inscription on the other side professes to have been set up by "Damasus, Bishop, to Eusebius, Bishop and Martyr," and to have been written by Furius Dionysius Filocalus, "a worshipper (*cultor*) and lover of Pope Damasus." But it is easy to see at a glance that it never was really executed by the same hand to which we are indebted for so many other beautiful productions of that Pope. At first, therefore, and whilst only a few fragments of this inscription had been recovered, De Rossi was tempted to conjecture that it might be one of the earliest efforts of the artist who subsequently attained such perfection. At length, however, the difficulty was solved in a more sure and satisfactory way. A diligent search in the earth with which the chamber was filled brought to light several fragments of the original stone, on which the letters are executed with the same faultlessness as on the other specimens of its class. The visitor to the Catacombs may see them painted, in a different colour from the rest, in the copy of the epitaph which De Rossi has caused to be affixed to the wall; and he will observe that amongst them are some letters which are wanting in the more ancient copy transcribed on the reverse of Caracalla's monument. It is clear that the original must have been broken in pieces, by the Lombards or other ancient plunderers of the Catacombs, and that the copy which we now see is one of the restorations by Pope Vigilus or some other Pontiff about that time (page 47). The copyist was so ignorant that he could only transcribe the letters which were on the spot before his eyes, and, even when he was conscious that a letter was missing, he could only leave a vacant space, being doubtful how it should be supplied. Witness the space left for the first letter of *Domino* in the penultimate line of the inscription, and the word *in* altogether omitted in the third line.

DAMASUS EPISCOPUS FECIT

HERACLIUS VETUIT LABSOS PECCATA DOLERE,

EUSEBIUS MISEROS DOCUIT SUA CRIMINA FLERE;

SCINDITUR IN PARTES POPULUS, GLISCENTE FURORE ;

SEDITIO, CÆDES, BELLUM, DISCORDIA, LITES ;

EXTEMPLO PARITER PULSI FERITATE TYRANNI,

INTEGRA CUM RECTOR SERVARET FŒDERA PACIS.

PERTULIT EXILIUM DOMINO SUB JUDICE LÆTUS

LITORE TRINACRIO MUNDUM VITAMQUE RELIQUIT.

EUSEBIO EPISCOPO ET MARTYRI.

"Heraclius forbad those who had fallen away [in times of persecution] to grieve for their sins.
But Eusebius taught those unhappy men to weep for their crimes.
The people are divided into parties; fury increases;
Sedition, murder, fighting, quarrelling, and strife.
Presently both [the Pope and the heretic] are exiled by the cruelty of the tyrant,
Although the Pope was preserving the bonds of peace inviolate.
He bore his exile with joy, looking to the Lord as his Judge,
And on the shore of Sicily gave up the world and his life."

Having sufficiently considered the *form* of the inscription, let us now say a few words about its *substance*, which is important, because it restores to us a lost chapter of Church history. Every student knows how keenly contested in the early ages of the Church was the question as to the discipline to be observed towards those Christians who relapsed into an outward profession of Paganism under the pressure of persecution. There were some who would fain close the door of reconciliation altogether against these unhappy men (*miseri*), whilst others claimed for them restitution of all Christian privileges before they had brought forth worthy fruits of penance.

The question arose whenever a persecution followed after a long term of peace; for during such a time men's minds were specially apt to decline from primitive fervour, and the number of the lapsed to increase. We are not surprised, therefore, to find the question agitated during the persecution of Decius in the middle of the third century. There is still extant a touching letter, written to St. Cyprian by the clergy of Rome at a time when the Holy See was vacant after the martyrdom of St. Fabian, which clearly defines the tradition and practice of the Church. In it they say that absolution was freely given to those of the lapsed who are in danger of death, but to others only when wholesome penance has been exacted; and they declare that "they have left nothing undone that the perverse may not boast of their being too easy, nor the true penitents accuse them of inflexible cruelty." The same question arose under the same circumstances in the persecution of Diocletian. Pope Marcellus was firm in upholding the Church's discipline, but he was resisted with such violence that public order was disturbed in the city by the strife of contending factions, and the Pope was banished by order of the Emperor Maxentius. This we learn from another inscription of Pope Damasus, who says that he wrote it in order that the faithful might not be ignorant of the merit of the holy Pontiff. Eusebius was the immediate successor of Marcellus, and the epitaph now before us is clearly a continuation of the same history, ending in the same punishment of the Pope, as the reward of his contention for the liberties of the Church. For it should be remembered that these Popes were driven from their see and died in exile, not because they refused to apostatize, but because they insisted on maintaining the integrity of ecclesiastical discipline. They may justly be reckoned, therefore, among the earliest of that noble army of martyrs, who, from those days even to our own, have braved every danger rather than consent to govern the Church in accordance with other than the Church's rules.

It yet remains to make two further remarks upon the epitaph of Pope Eusebius before we leave it. The first is, that he is called a martyr, though it nowhere appears that he really shed his blood; but this is by no means the only instance in which the title of martyr is given in ancient documents to men who have suffered for the faith and died whilst those sufferings continued. And secondly, it is to be observed that although we have no record of the translation of the body of St. Eusebius from Sicily to Rome, there is no reason to doubt the fact. All the earliest monuments speak of him as buried in a crypt of the Cemetery of St. Callixtus, and although the law forbad the translation of the bodies of those who had died in exile unless the emperor's permission had been previously obtained, the old lawyers tell us that this permission was freely given. Numerous examples teach us the great anxiety of the ancient churches to have their bishops buried in the midst of them; no doubt, therefore, the necessary permission was asked for, as soon as a change in the imperial policy towards the Church made it possible; and the body of St. Eusebius was recovered and brought to Rome soon after his death, just as that of one of his predecessors, St. Pontian, had been brought from Sardinia by St. Fabian.

CHAPTER IV.

THE TOMB OF ST. CORNELIUS.

WE have not promised to conduct the visitor to everything that is worth seeing in this cemetery, but only to enumerate and explain the principal monuments of historical importance which every stranger usually sees. And the only specimen of this class which remains to be spoken of is the tomb of St. Cornelius, which lies some way off. In order to reach it we must traverse a vast network of galleries, narrow and irregular, connecting what were once independent cemeteries, or at least were *arcæ* added at various times to the Cemetery of Callixtus. If our guide is not in too great haste, he may allow us to step aside into two or three chambers by the way, in which are certain objects of interest worth looking at. The first is a long inscription belonging to the last decade of the third century, in which the Deacon Severus records that he has obtained leave from the Pope Marcellinus to make a double chamber, with *arcosolia* and a *luminare,* in which himself and his family may have quiet graves (*mansionem in pace quietam*). This is in the third area of the cemetery, next to the area in which we visited the crypt of St. Eusebius.

In the adjoining area, and belonging probably to the same date, is a very curious fresco, much damaged by having been cut through for the sake of making a grave behind it, yet still easily distinguishable in all its main features. The Good Shepherd occupies the centre of the painting. On either side is an apostle, probably SS. Peter and Paul, hastening away from Christ, Who has sent them to go and teach all nations. These are represented by two sheep standing before each of the apostles; and over their heads hangs a rock, whence pour down streams of water, which the apostles are receiving in their hands and turning on the heads of the sheep. We need no special explanation of this; we have already learnt that the Rock is Christ, and that the waters represent all Christian graces and sacraments. But what is worth noticing in this picture is the various attitudes of the sheep, and the corresponding distribution of the water. A perfect torrent is falling on the animal that stands with outstretched neck and head uplifted, drinking in all he hears with simplicity and eagerness; whilst another, which has turned its back upon the apostle, is left without any water at all. Of the other two, one is standing with head downcast, as if in doubt and perplexity, and upon him too grace is still being poured out more abundantly than upon the fourth, which is eating grass, *i.e.*, occupied with the affairs of this world.

On the right hand side of this *arcosolium* are two representations of Moses; in the one he is striking the rock, and one of the Jews is catching some of the water which gushes forth; in the other he is taking off his shoes, preparing to obey the summons of God, who is represented by a hand coming forth from the cloud. The painting on the other side of the *arcosolium* is even more defaced than that in the centre. A large semi-circular recess has been cut through it, and then the smoke of the lamp which burnt in this recess during the fourth and fifth centuries has almost obliterated the little that remained of the figure of our Lord. He stood between two of His apostles, who are offering Him bread and fish, and six baskets of loaves stand on the ground before them.

And now we will not linger any more upon the road, but follow our guide, who hurries forward along the intricate passages until he lands us at last in an irregularly shaped space, illuminated by a *luminare*, decorated with paintings, and bearing manifest tokens of having been once a great centre of devotion. There is the pillar to support the usual vessel of oil or more precious unguents to be burnt before the tomb of the martyr; and hard by is a gravestone let into the wall with the words CORNELIUS MARTYR, EP.

The stone does not close one of the common graves such as are seen in the walls of the galleries or of the *cubicula*, neither is the grave an ordinary *arcosolium*. The lower part of it, indeed, resembles an *arcosolium* inasmuch as it is large enough to contain three or four bodies, but there is no arch over it. The opening is rectangular, not circular, and yet there is no trace of any slab having been let into the wall to cover the top of the grave. It is probable, therefore, that a sarcophagus once filled the vacant space, and that the top of this sarcophagus served as the *mensa* or altar, an arrangement of which other examples have been found.

But how came Pope Cornelius to be buried here, and not with his predecessors in the Papal Crypt? He was Pope, A.D. 250, between Fabian and Lucius, both of whom were buried, as we have seen, in that crypt. It is to be observed, however, that Cornelius is the only Pope, during the first three centuries, who bore the name of a noble Roman family; and many ancient epitaphs have been found in the area round this tomb, of persons who belonged to the same family. It is obvious, therefore, to conjecture that this sepulchre was the private property of some branch of the Gens Cornelia. The public Cemetery of St. Callixtus may have been closed at this time by order of the Government; but even without such a reason, it may have been the wish of the family that the Pope should not be separated in burial from the rest of his race. The same circumstance would account for the epitaph being written in Latin, not in Greek, for many of the old patrician families clung to the language of their forefathers long after the use of Greek had come into fashion; and this departure from the official language of the Church (for such, in fact, Greek really was at that time) is quite of a piece with the preference of the domestic to the official burial-place.

But whatever may be the true explanation of these circumstances, the fact is at least certain that Cornelius was buried here; and above and below the opening of his tomb are fragments, still adhering to the wall, of large slabs of marble, containing a few letters of what were once important inscriptions. The upper inscription was unquestionably the work of Damasus. The letters of the lower, though closely resembling the Damasine type, yet present a few points of difference—sufficient to warrant the conjecture of De Rossi that they were executed by the same hand, but with slight variations, in order to mark that it belonged to another series of monuments. We subjoin a copy of both inscriptions, in the form in which De Rossi believes them to have been originally written. In the first inscription the difference of type will distinguish the earlier half of each line, which is a conjectural restoration, from the latter half which still remains *in situ;* and in estimating the degree of probability of the restorations, the reader should bear in mind two things: *first*, that the Damasine inscriptions were engraved with such mathematical precision that no emendations are admissible which would materially increase or diminish the number of letters in each line; and *secondly*, that whereas Damasus was in the habit of repeating himself very frequently in his epitaphs, several of De Rossi's restorations are mere literal reproductions of some of his favourite forms of speech. Had the following epitaph been found in some ancient MS., and there attributed to Pope Damasus, we are confident that no critic would have seen reason to doubt its genuineness :—

>ASPICE, DESCENSU EXSTRUCTO TENEBRISQUE FUGATIS,
>CORNELI MONUMENTA VIDES TUMULUMQUE SACRATUM.
>HOC OPUS ÆGROTI DAMASI PRÆSTANTIA FECIT,
>ESSET UT ACCESSUS MELIOR, POPULISQUE PARATUM
>AUXILIUM SANCTI, ET VALEAS SI FUNDERE PURO
>CORDE PRECES, DAMASUS MELIOR CONSURGERE POSSET,
>QUEM NON LUCIS AMOR, TENUIT MAGE CURA LABORIS.

"Behold, a new staircase having been made, and the darkness put to flight,
You see the monuments of Cornelius and his sacred tomb.
This work the zeal of Damasus has accomplished, at a time when he was sick ;
That so the means of approach might be better, and the aid of the saint
Put more within the reach of the people ; and that if you pour forth prayers
From a pure heart, Damasus may rise up in better health ;
Though it has not been love of life, but rather anxiety for work, that has retained him in this life."

The second inscription De Rossi would restore as follows :—

>SIRICIUS PERFECIT OPUS,
>CONCLUSIT ET ARCAM
>MARMORE, CORNELI QUONIAM
>PIA MEMBRA RETENTAT

—that is to say, he supposes that, Damasus having died, his successor Siricius completed the work that had been begun, and, furthermore, strengthened the wall which enclosed the tomb of St. Cornelius with this very thick slab of marble—a work which may have been rendered necessary by the alterations already made by Damasus. Of course, these restorations of the mutilated inscriptions must always remain more or less doubtful, for we fear there is no chance of any other fragments of the original ever coming to light. We publish them under the same reserve with which he himself proposes them, as at least approximations to the truth. He says that, without daring to affirm their literal correctness, there are certainly strong reasons for believing that they exactly reproduce the sense of the original.

This same tomb of St. Cornelius will supply us with an example of De Rossi's power of happy conjecture, confirmed with absolute certainty by subsequent discoveries. He had often publicly expressed his confident expectation of finding at this tomb of St. Cornelius some memorial of his cotemporary, St. Cyprian. These two saints were martyred on the same day, though in different years; and their feasts were, therefore, always celebrated together, just as they are now, on the 16th of September, all the liturgical prayers for the day being common to both. Now, De Rossi had found in one of the old Itineraries, to whose accuracy of detail he had been greatly indebted, an extraordinary misstatement, viz., that the bodies of both these saints rested together in the same catacomb, whereas everybody knows that St. Cyprian was buried in Africa. He conjectured, therefore, that the pilgrim had been led into this blunder by something he had seen at the tomb of St. Cornelius. On its rediscovery, the cause of the error stands at once revealed. Immediately on the right hand side of the grave are two large figures of bishops painted on the wall, with a legend by the side of each, declaring them to be St. Cornelius and St. Cyprian.

On the other side of the tomb is another painting, executed in the same style, on the wall at the end of the gallery: two figures of bishops, again designated by their proper names and titles. Only one of these can now be deciphered, SCS XUSTUS PP ROM, *i.e.*, Pope Sixtus II., of whose connection with this cemetery we have already heard so often. The other name began with an O, and was probably St. Optatus, an African bishop and martyr, whose body had been brought to Rome and buried in this cemetery.

These paintings are manifestly a late work: perhaps they were executed in the days of Leo III., A.D. 795-815, of whom it is recorded in the *Liber Pontificalis*, that "he renewed the Cemetery of Sts. Sixtus and Cornelius on the Appian Way;" and the legend which runs round them would have a special significance as the motto of one who had been almost miraculously delivered out of the hands of his enemies by the Emperor Charlemagne. It is taken from the 17th verse of the 58th Psalm: "Ego autem cantabo virtutem Tuam et exaltabo misericordiam Tuam quia factus es et susceptor meus." ...

"I will sing Thy strength, and will extol Thy mercy, for Thou art become my support." Of course, this had not been the earliest ornamentation of these walls. Even now, we can detect traces of a more ancient painting, and of *graffiti* upon it, underlying this later work. The *graffiti* are only the names of priests and deacons, who either came here to offer the holy sacrifice, or perhaps to take part in the translation of the relics: "*Leo prb., Theodorus prb., Kiprianus Diaconus,*" &c.

We are drawing very near to the end of our subterranean walk: indeed, the staircase which is to restore us to the upper air close to the very entrance of the vineyard is immediately behind us, as we stand contemplating the tomb of St. Cornelius. Nevertheless, if we are not too weary, nor our guide too impatient, we should do well to resist the temptation to escape, until we have first visited two small chambers which are in the immediate neighbourhood. They contain some of the most ancient specimens of painting to be found in the whole range of the Catacombs. The ceilings are divided into circles and other geometrical figures, and then the spaces are filled up with graceful arabesques, birds, and flowers, peacocks, and dancing genii. It was the sight of such paintings as these which led the Protestant writer quoted in a former chapter to express an opinion that, on first entering some of the decorated chambers in the Catacombs, it is not easy to determine whether the work is Christian or Pagan. Here, indeed, the Good

Shepherd in one centre and Daniel between two lions in the other soon solve the doubt; but all the other details and the excellence of their execution may well have suggested it. No one can doubt that the paintings belong to the very earliest period of Christian art, when the forms and traditions of the classical age had not yet died away.

In the first of the two chambers we are speaking of, there is nothing special to be seen besides the ceiling; but the second and more distant is more richly decorated. Here, two sepulchral chambers open one into the other: over the doorway which admits to the inner vault is represented the Baptism of our Lord by St. John: He is coming up out of the water and the dove is descending upon Him. On the wall opposite to the entrance is that fish carrying the basket of bread and wine that has been already described (page 81). On the wall to the left is a pail of milk standing on a kind of altar between two sheep, and we know from St. Irenæus and from some of the earliest and most authentic acts of the martyrs that milk was an accepted symbol of the Holy Eucharist. Opposite to this are doves and trees, which are often used as types of the souls of the blessed in Paradise. Thus, on one side we have the faithful on earth standing around the Divine food which prepares for heaven; and on the other, souls released from the prison of the body have flown away and are at rest, reposing amid the joys of another world; so that it would almost seem as though the same sequence of ideas presided over the decoration of these chambers, as was certainly present to the minds of those who designed the ornamentation of the sacramental chambers in the Cemetery of St. Callixtus (page 84).

And now at length we must conclude our visit to St. Callixtus. We fear that we have already enumerated more than can be seen with advantage during the course of a single visit; yet it is worth an effort to see it all, because it includes monuments which illustrate nearly every century of the period during which the Catacombs were used. It is for this reason that a visit to St. Callixtus is so singularly valuable, whether it be intended to take this cemetery as a sample of all, or only to use it as an introduction to others. Those who propose to pursue the subject further would do well to visit next the Catacomb of SS. Nereus and Achilles, which lies at no great distance, off the Via Ardeatina; then the Cemetery of Pretextatus on the other side of the Via Appia; and finally, the *Cœmeterium Ostrianum* on the Via Nomentana. When these have been carefully examined, there will still remain many interesting monuments, of considerable historical importance, in other less famous cemeteries; but enough will have been seen to give an excellent general acquaintance with the main characteristics of Roma Sotterranea.

www.ingramcontent.com/pod-product-compliance
Lightning Source LLC
Chambersburg PA
CBHW031443160426
43195CB00010BB/825